NOWHERE MAN

Published by Forward Comix

Forward Comix
467 Bay Ridge PKWY, Brooklyn, NY 11209
Designed in part by The Blue Griffin

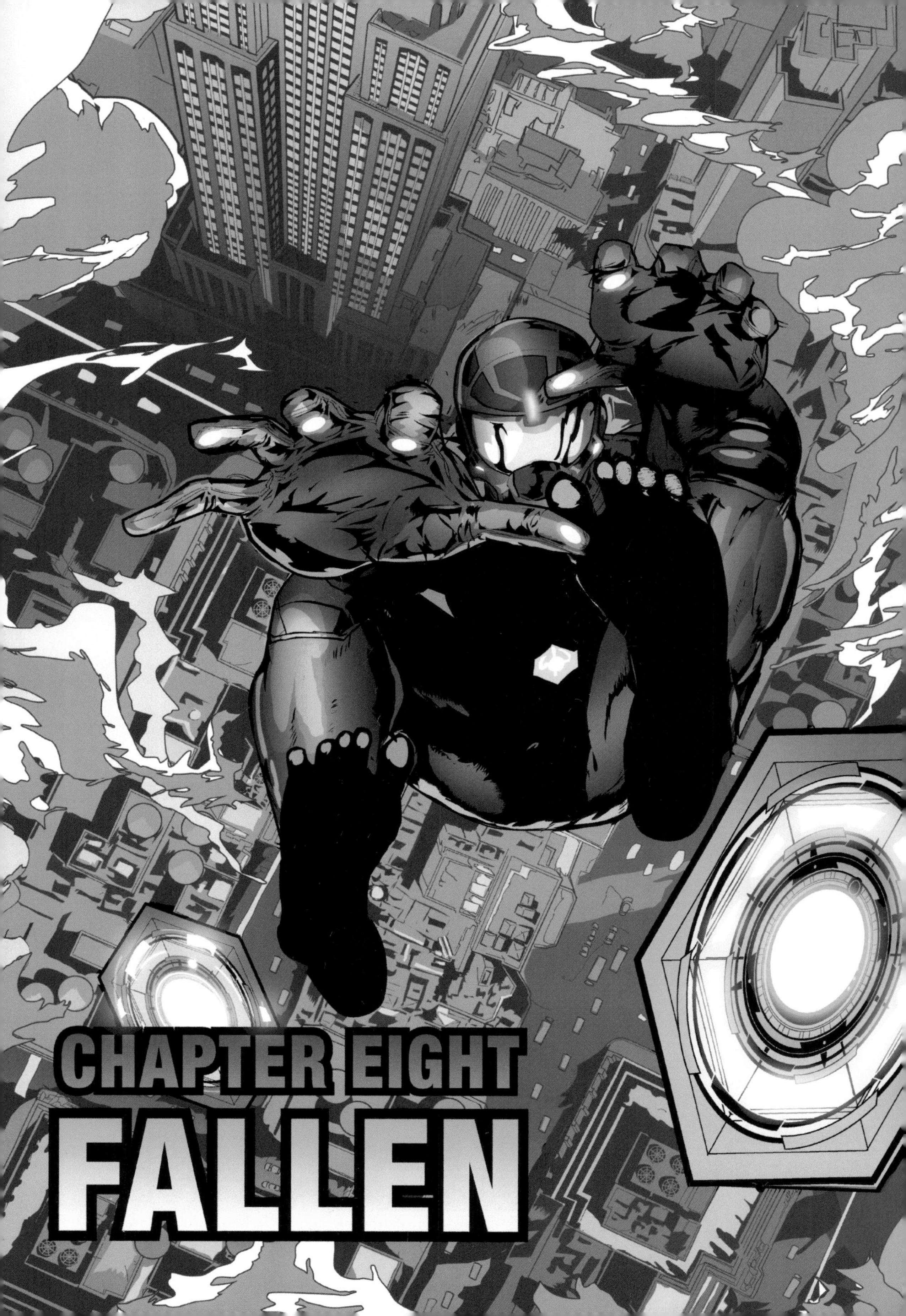
CHAPTER EIGHT
FALLEN

EXECUTING THIS MANEUVER DIFFICULT BUT NOT IMPOSSIBLE.

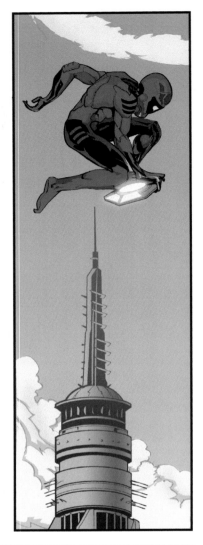

SYSTEM FAILURE...

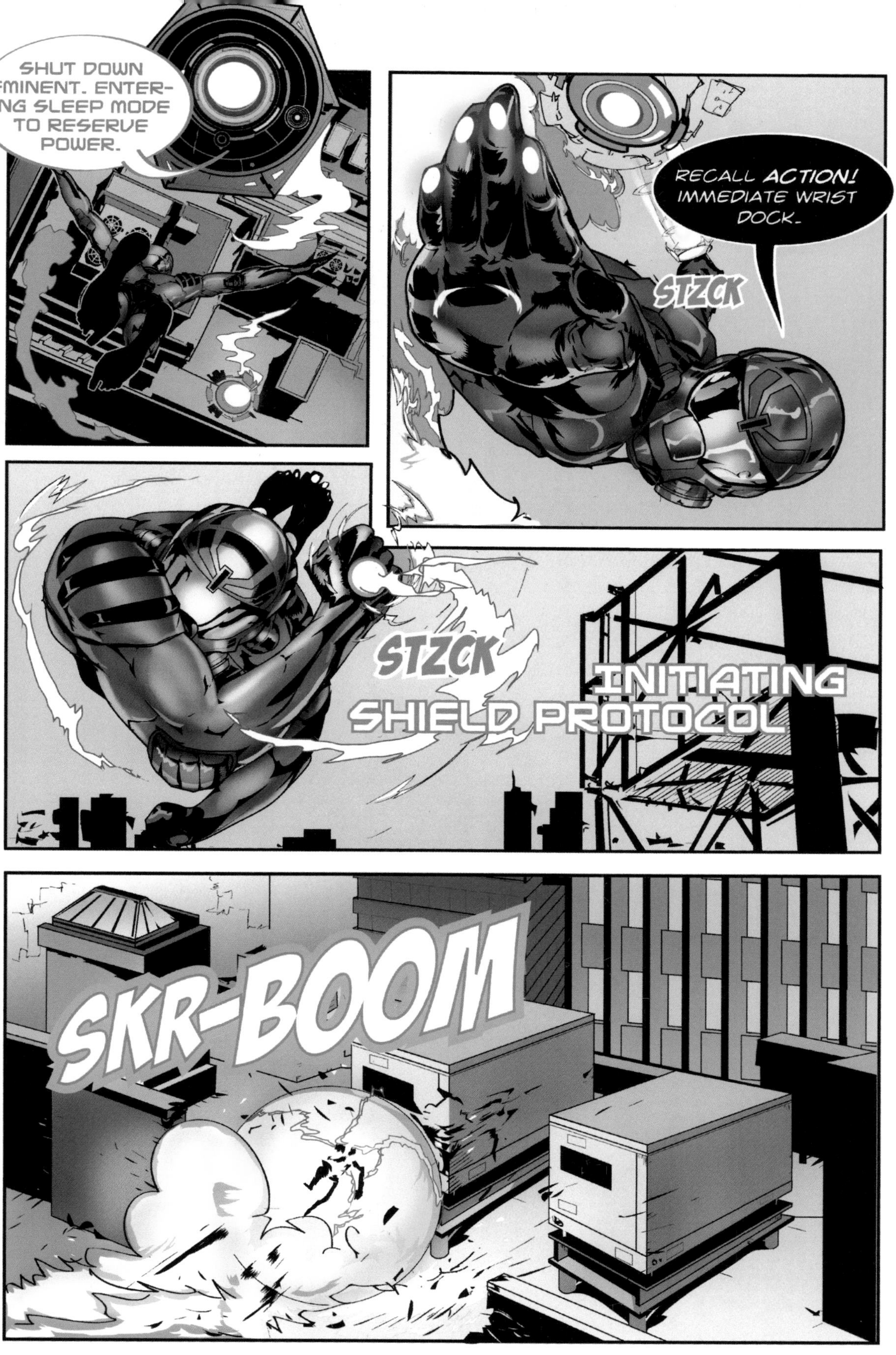

SHUT DOWN EMINENT. ENTERING SLEEP MODE TO RESERVE POWER.
RECALL ACTION! IMMEDIATE WRIST DOCK.
STZCK
STZCK
INITIATING SHIELD PROTOCOL
SKR-BOOM

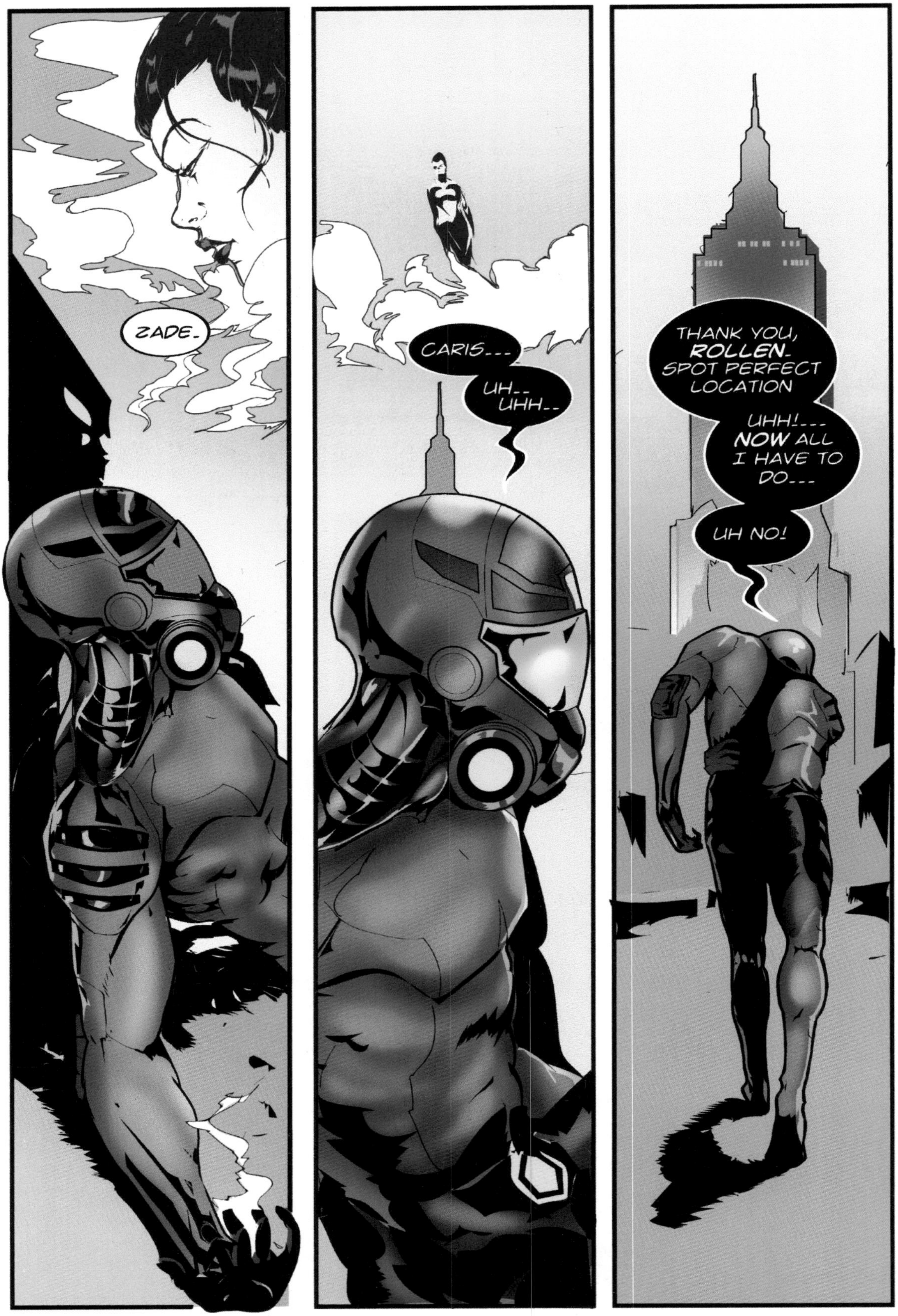
ZADE-
CARIS---
UH--
UHH--
THANK YOU, ROLLEN- SPOT PERFECT LOCATION
UHH!--- NOW ALL I HAVE TO DO---
UH NO!

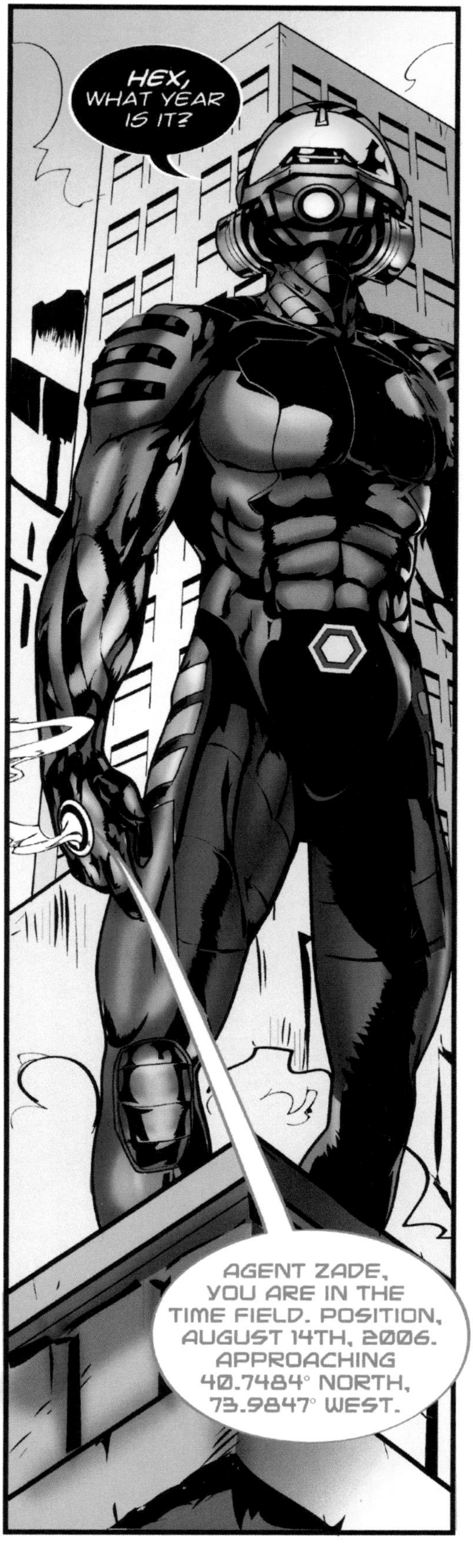
HEX, WHAT YEAR IS IT?
AGENT ZADE, YOU ARE IN THE TIME FIELD. POSITION, AUGUST 14TH, 2006. APPROACHING 40.7484° NORTH, 73.9847° WEST.

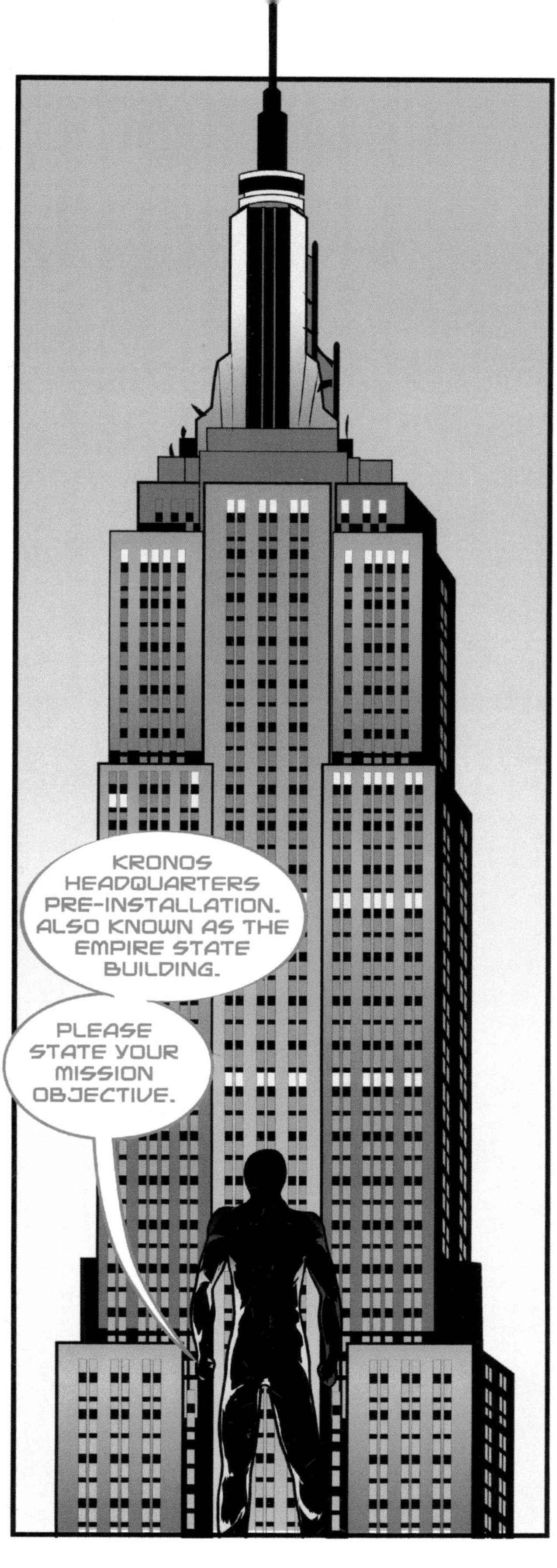
KRONOS HEADQUARTERS PRE-INSTALLATION. ALSO KNOWN AS THE EMPIRE STATE BUILDING.
PLEASE STATE YOUR MISSION OBJECTIVE.

VOLUME 01: YOU DON'T KNOW JACK

PART 03

**WRITTEN AND ILLUSTRATED BY
JEROME WALFORD**

EDITING
MAYA ROCK
RUSS LANE
AMY WALFORD

DEDICATED TO:
Amy Walford and our three rascals: Kayla, Charles and Colette.
Anything is possible.

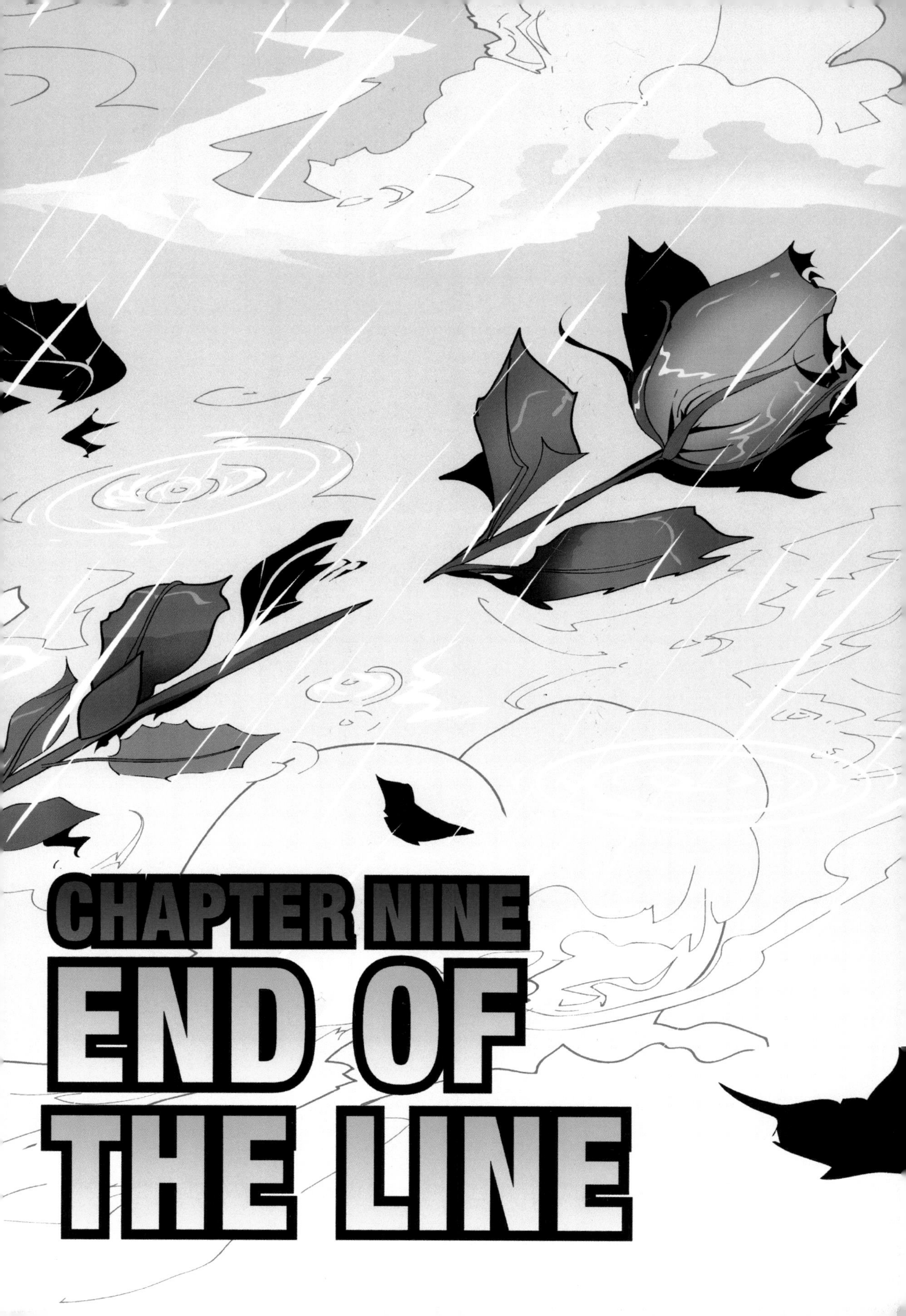
CHAPTER NINE
END OF
THE LINE

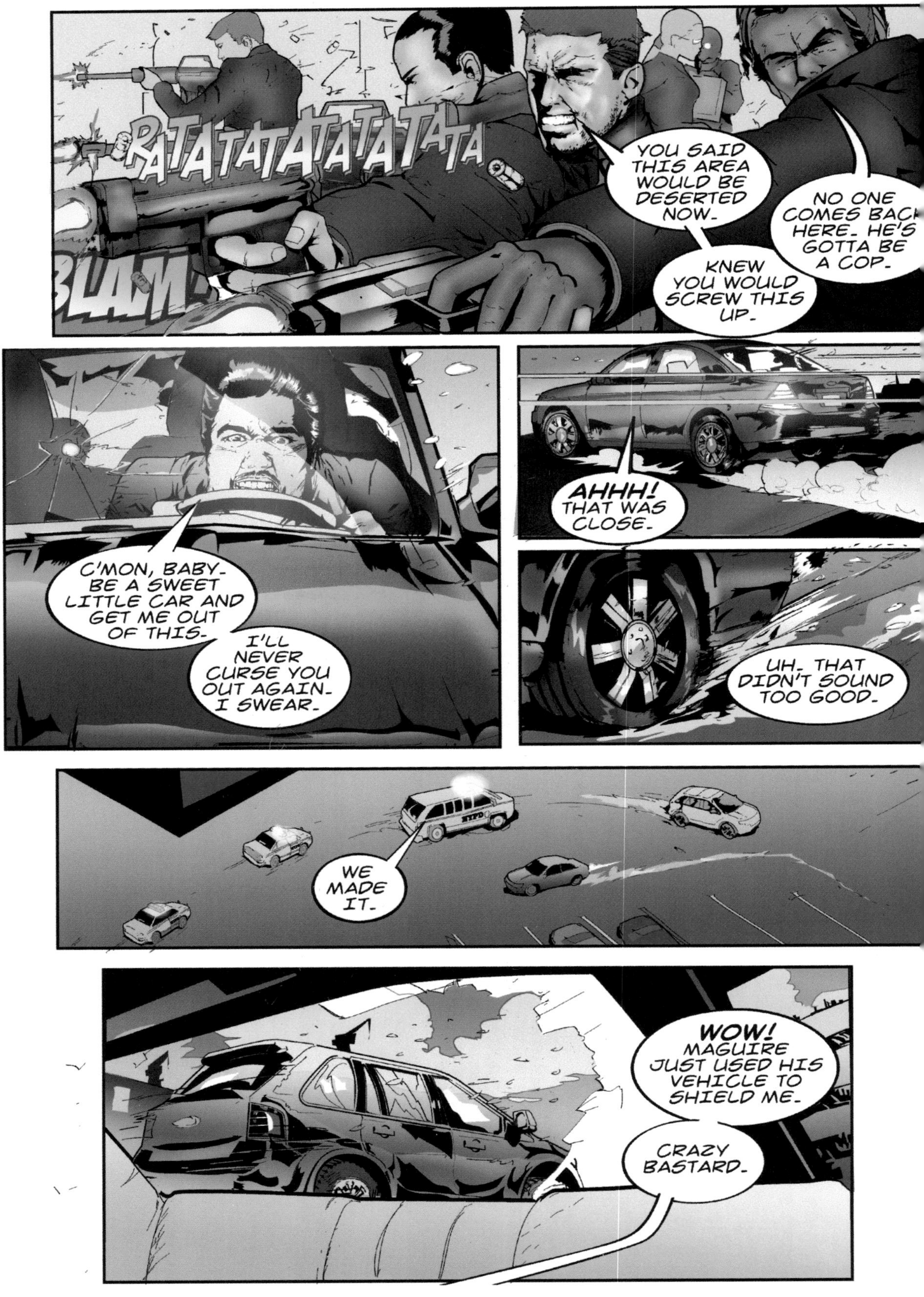
RATATATATATATATA
BLAM
YOU SAID THIS AREA WOULD BE DESERTED NOW.
KNEW YOU WOULD SCREW THIS UP.
NO ONE COMES BACK HERE. HE'S GOTTA BE A COP.
C'MON, BABY. BE A SWEET LITTLE CAR AND GET ME OUT OF THIS.
I'LL NEVER CURSE YOU OUT AGAIN. I SWEAR.
AHHH! THAT WAS CLOSE.
UH. THAT DIDN'T SOUND TOO GOOD.
NYPD
WE MADE IT.
WOW! MAGUIRE JUST USED HIS VEHICLE TO SHIELD ME.
CRAZY BASTARD.

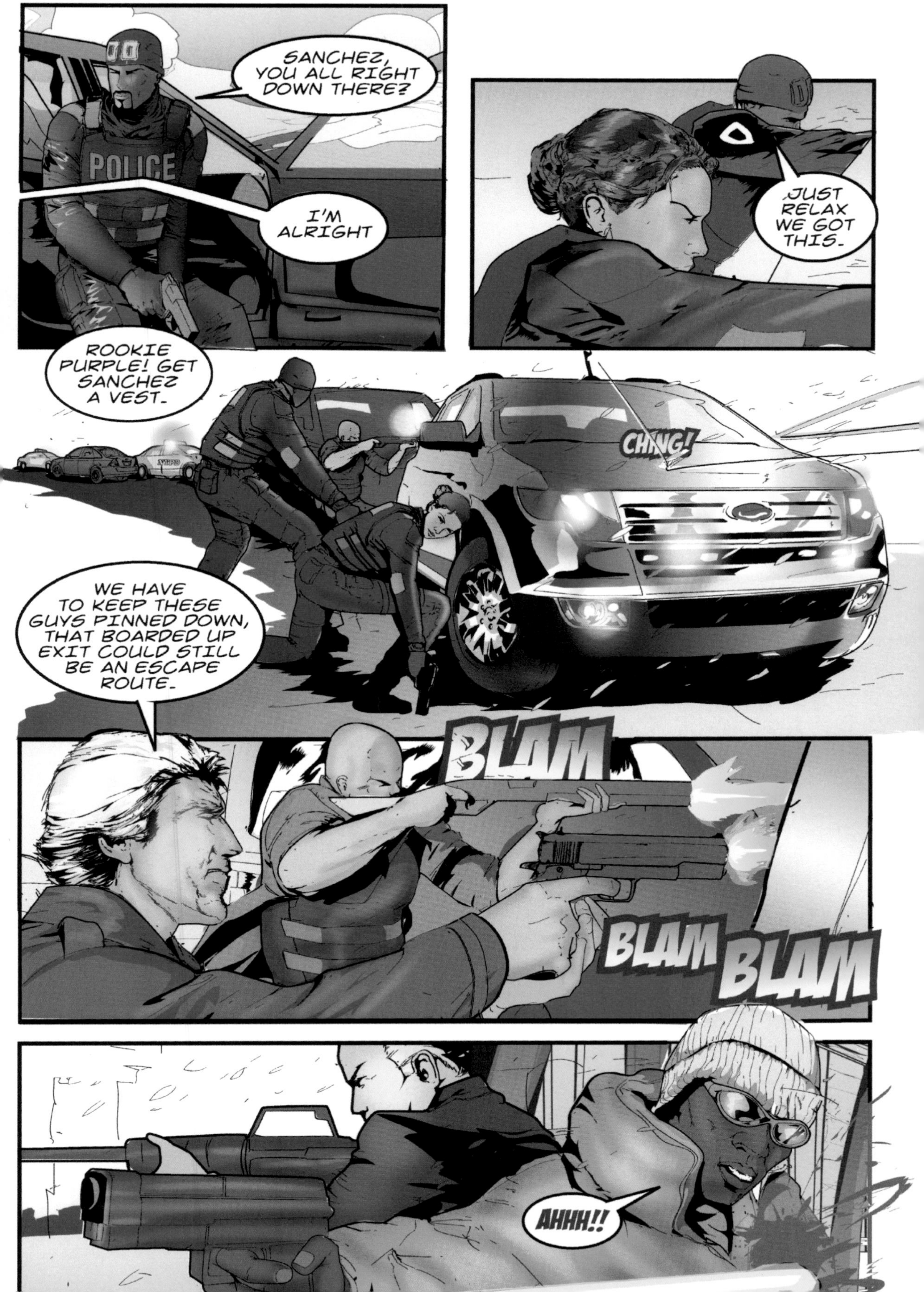
SANCHEZ, YOU ALL RIGHT DOWN THERE?
I'M ALRIGHT
JUST RELAX WE GOT THIS.
ROOKIE PURPLE! GET SANCHEZ A VEST.
CHING!
WE HAVE TO KEEP THESE GUYS PINNED DOWN, THAT BOARDED UP EXIT COULD STILL BE AN ESCAPE ROUTE.
BLAM
BLAM
BLAM
AHHH!!

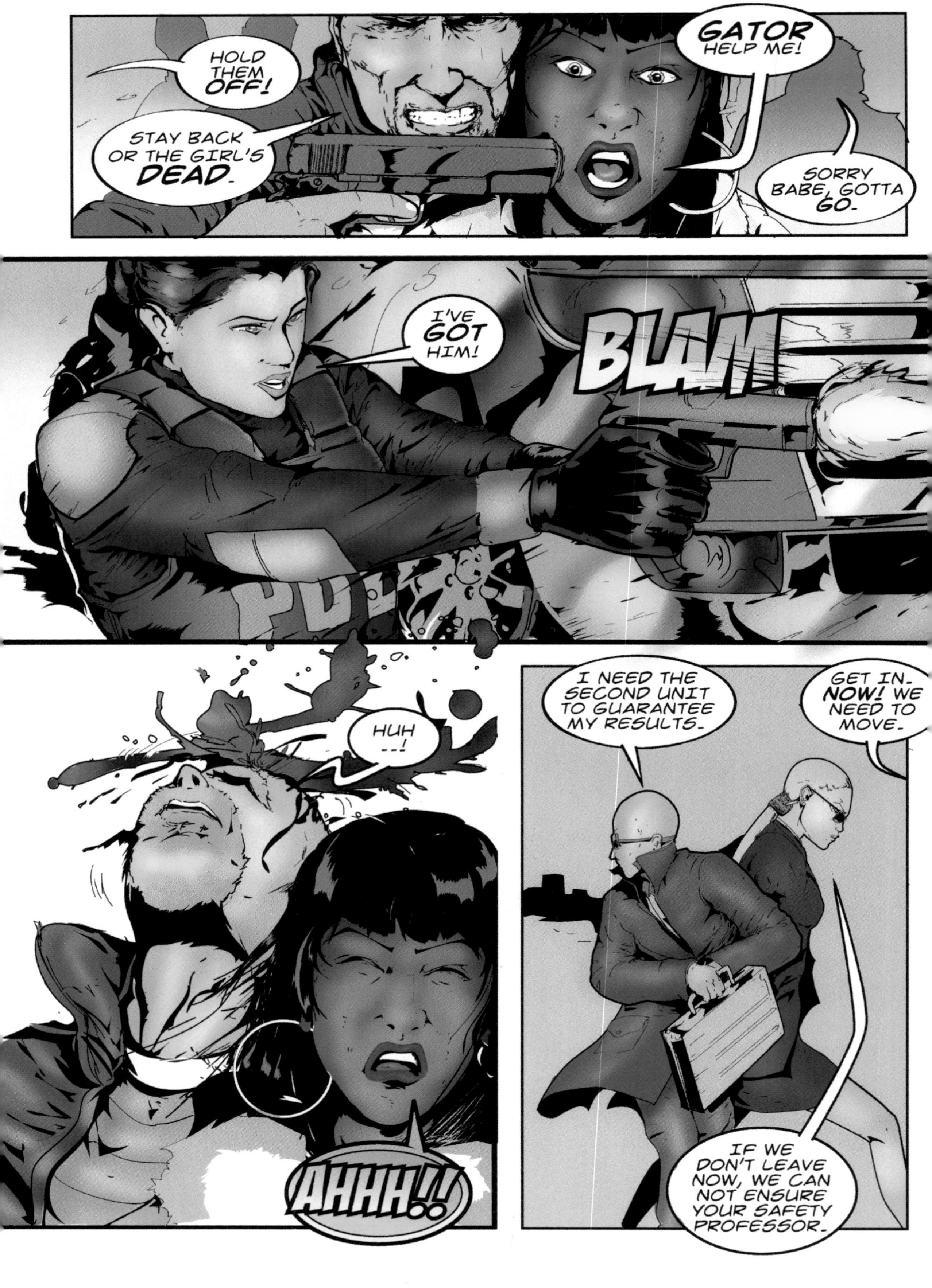
HOLD THEM OFF!
STAY BACK OR THE GIRL'S DEAD.
GATOR HELP ME!
SORRY BABE, GOTTA GO.
I'VE GOT HIM!
BLAM
HUH --!
AHHH!!!
I NEED THE SECOND UNIT TO GUARANTEE MY RESULTS.
GET IN. NOW! WE NEED TO MOVE.
IF WE DON'T LEAVE NOW, WE CAN NOT ENSURE YOUR SAFETY PROFESSOR.

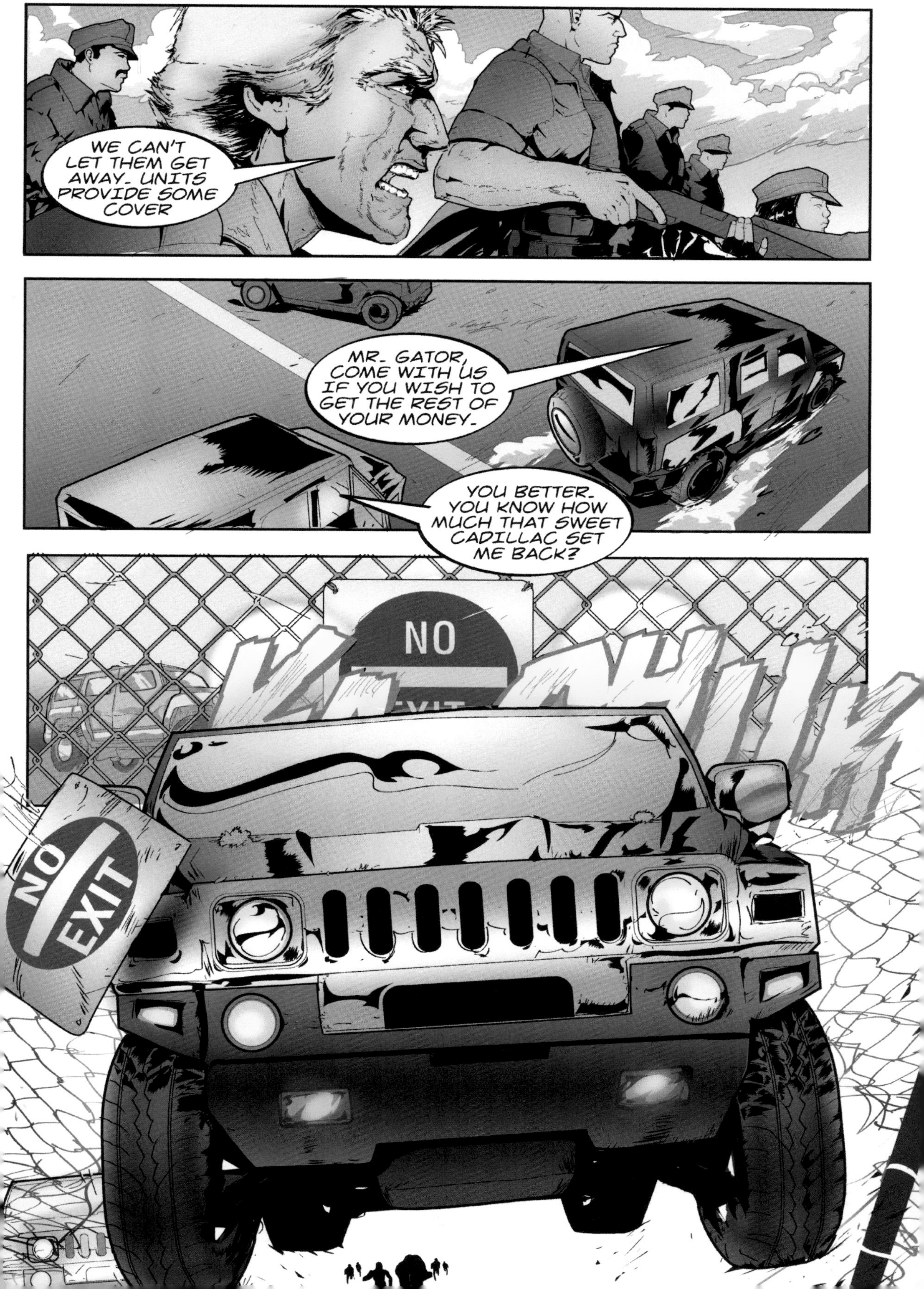
WE CAN'T LET THEM GET AWAY. UNITS PROVIDE SOME COVER
MR. GATOR, COME WITH US IF YOU WISH TO GET THE REST OF YOUR MONEY.
YOU BETTER. YOU KNOW HOW MUCH THAT SWEET CADILLAC SET ME BACK?
NO
NO EXIT

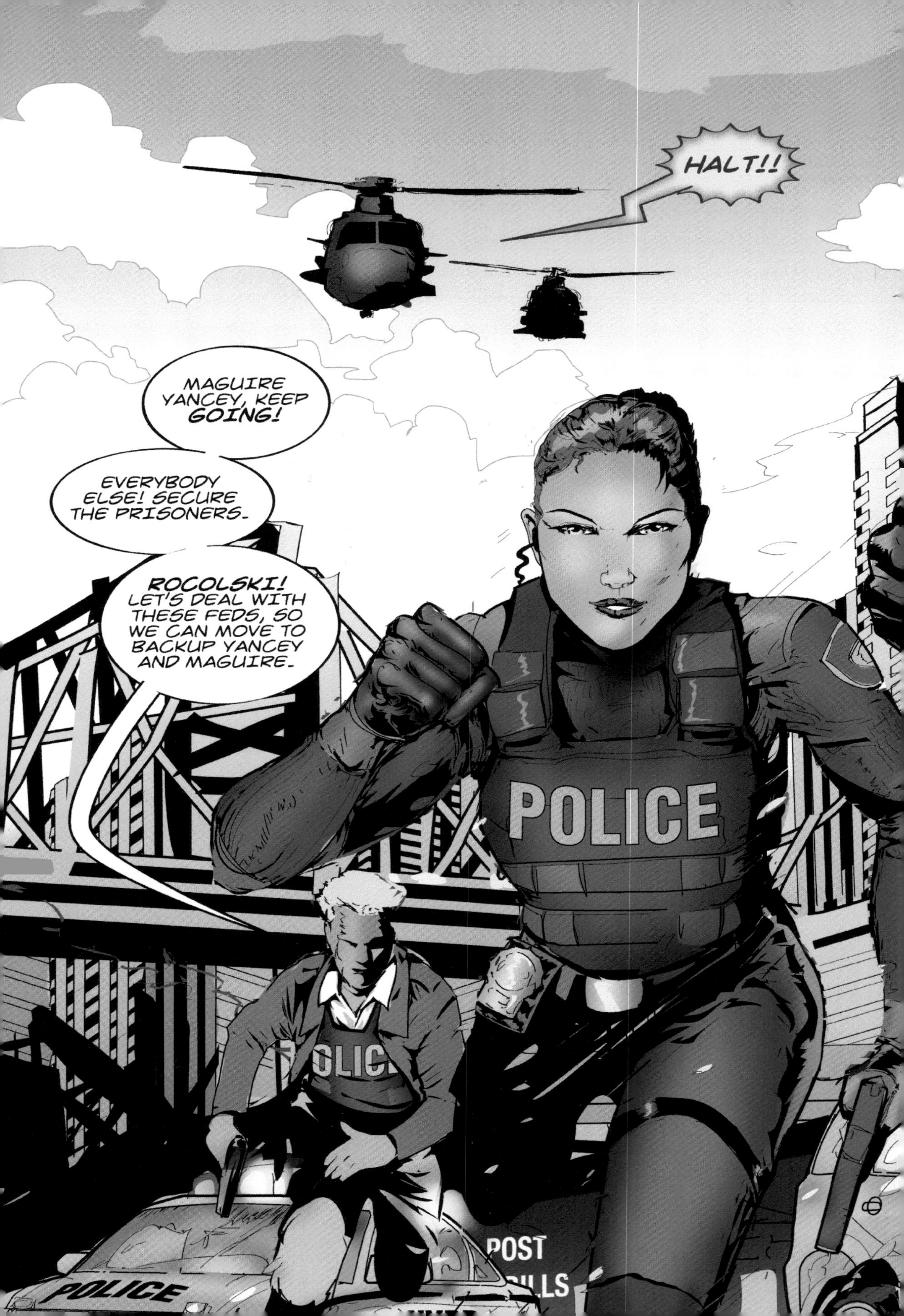
HALT!!
MAGUIRE YANCEY, KEEP GOING!
EVERYBODY ELSE! SECURE THE PRISONERS.
ROCOLSKI! LET'S DEAL WITH THESE FEDS, SO WE CAN MOVE TO BACKUP YANCEY AND MAGUIRE.
POLICE
POLICE
POLICE
POST

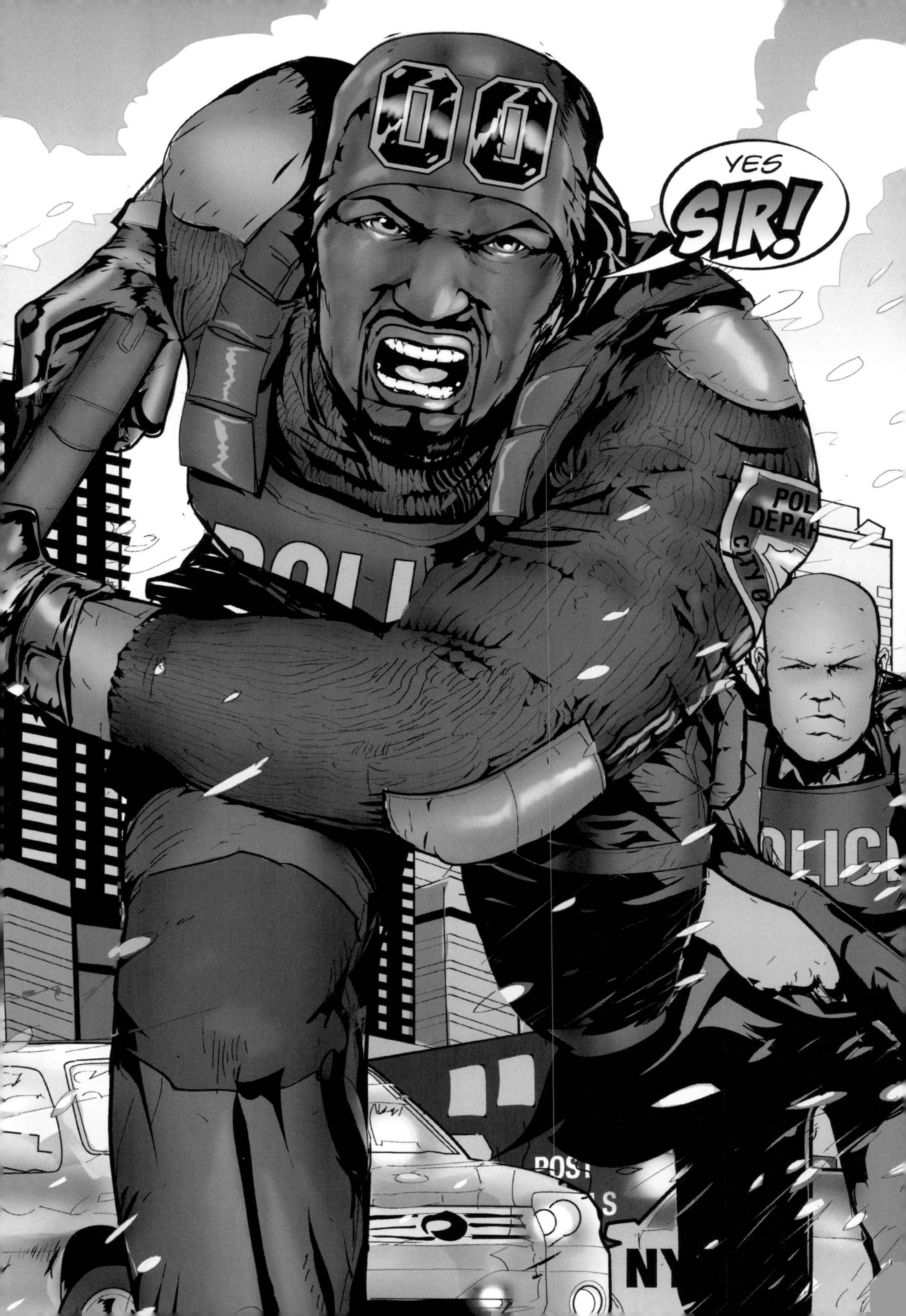
YES SIR!

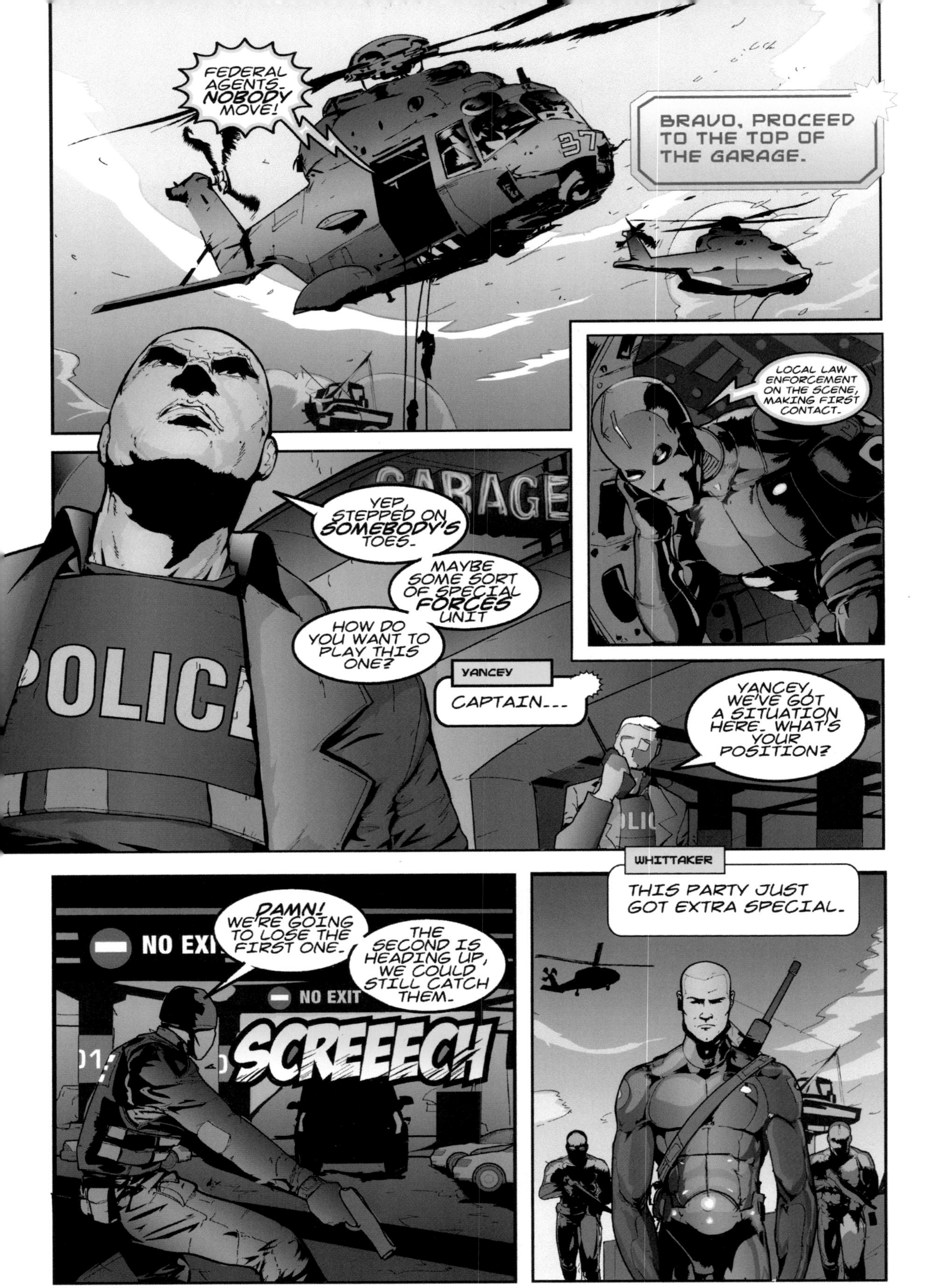
FEDERAL AGENTS- NOBODY MOVE!
BRAVO, PROCEED TO THE TOP OF THE GARAGE.
LOCAL LAW ENFORCEMENT ON THE SCENE, MAKING FIRST CONTACT.
GARAGE
YEP, STEPPED ON SOMEBODY'S TOES.
MAYBE SOME SORT OF SPECIAL FORCES UNIT
HOW DO YOU WANT TO PLAY THIS ONE?
POLICE
YANCEY
CAPTAIN...
YANCEY, WE'VE GOT A SITUATION HERE. WHAT'S YOUR POSITION?
NO EXIT
NO EXIT
DAMN! WE'RE GOING TO LOSE THE FIRST ONE.
THE SECOND IS HEADING UP, WE COULD STILL CATCH THEM.
SCREEECH
WHITTAKER
THIS PARTY JUST GOT EXTRA SPECIAL.

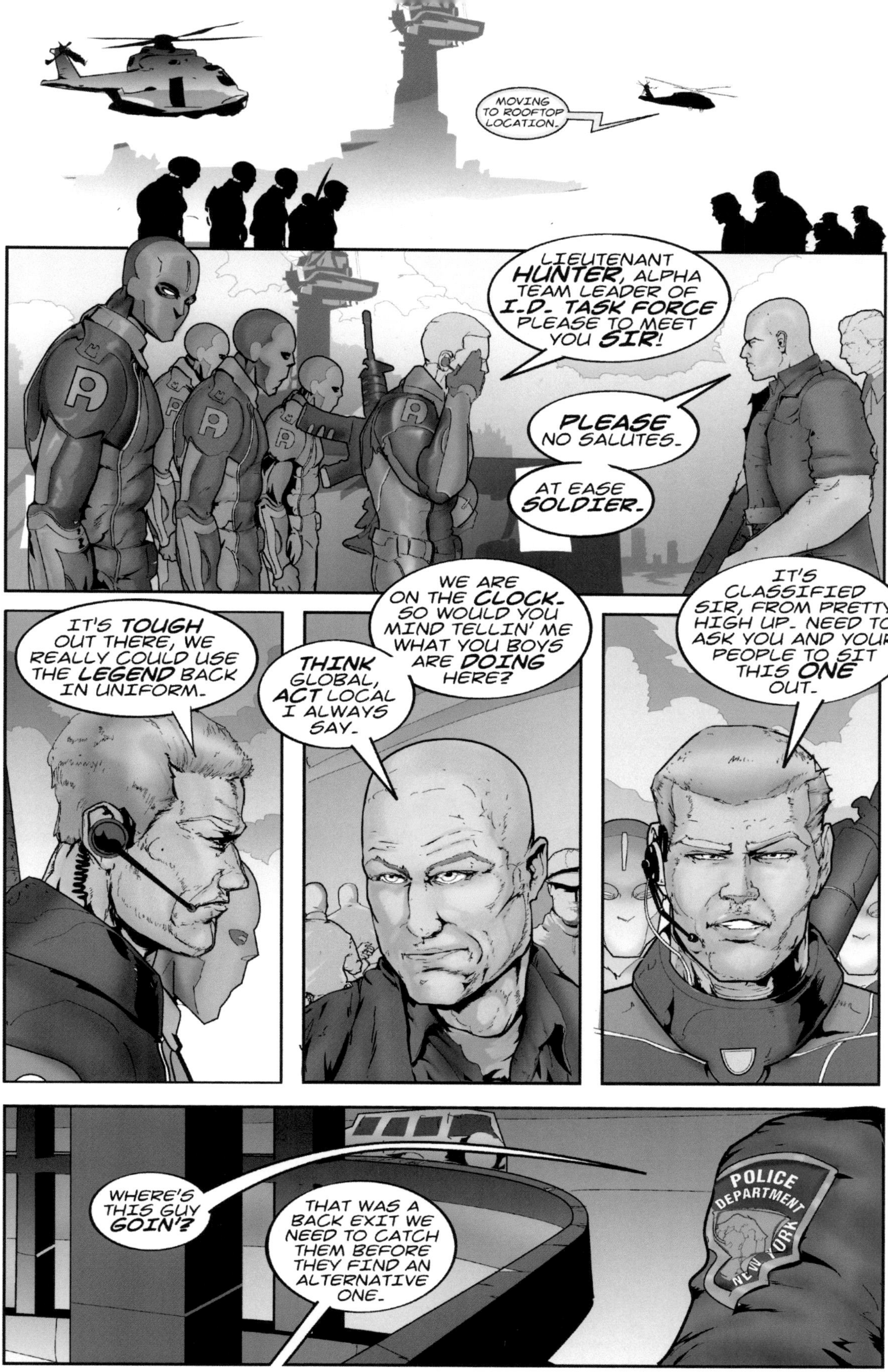
MOVING TO ROOFTOP LOCATION.
LIEUTENANT HUNTER, ALPHA TEAM LEADER OF I.D. TASK FORCE PLEASE TO MEET YOU SIR!
PLEASE NO SALUTES.
AT EASE SOLDIER.
IT'S TOUGH OUT THERE, WE REALLY COULD USE THE LEGEND BACK IN UNIFORM.
THINK GLOBAL, ACT LOCAL I ALWAYS SAY.
WE ARE ON THE CLOCK. SO WOULD YOU MIND TELLIN' ME WHAT YOU BOYS ARE DOING HERE?
IT'S CLASSIFIED SIR, FROM PRETTY HIGH UP. NEED TO ASK YOU AND YOUR PEOPLE TO SIT THIS ONE OUT.
POLICE DEPARTMENT NEW YORK
WHERE'S THIS GUY GOIN'?
THAT WAS A BACK EXIT WE NEED TO CATCH THEM BEFORE THEY FIND AN ALTERNATIVE ONE.

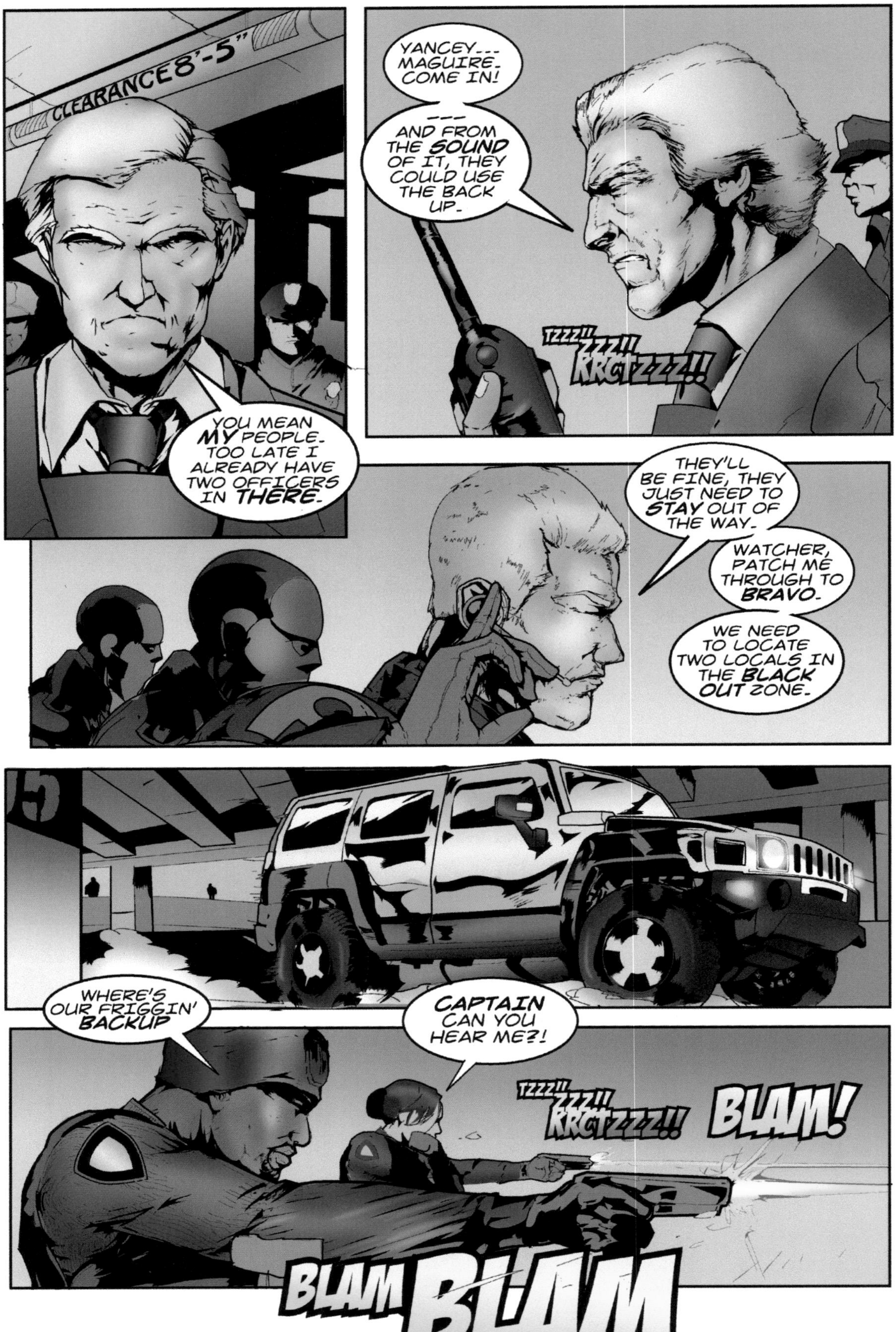
CLEARANCE 8'-5"
YOU MEAN MY PEOPLE. TOO LATE I ALREADY HAVE TWO OFFICERS IN THERE.
YANCEY... MAGUIRE. COME IN!
...AND FROM THE SOUND OF IT, THEY COULD USE THE BACK UP.
TZZZ!! ZZZ!! KRCTZZZ!!
THEY'LL BE FINE, THEY JUST NEED TO STAY OUT OF THE WAY.
WATCHER, PATCH ME THROUGH TO BRAVO.
WE NEED TO LOCATE TWO LOCALS IN THE BLACK OUT ZONE.
WHERE'S OUR FRIGGIN' BACKUP
CAPTAIN CAN YOU HEAR ME?!
TZZZ!! ZZZ!! KRCTZZZ!!
BLAM!
BLAM BLAM

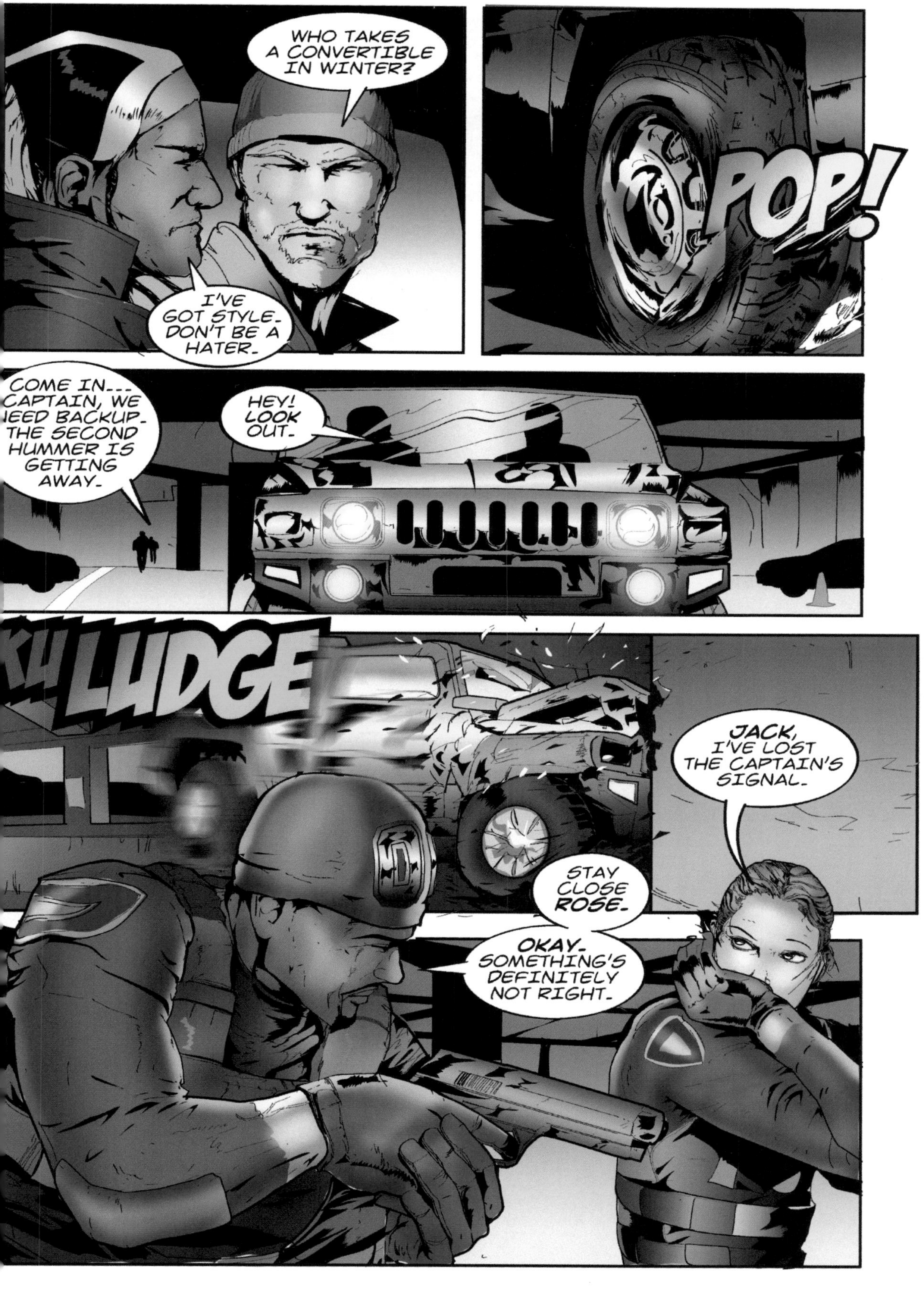
WHO TAKES A CONVERTIBLE IN WINTER?
I'VE GOT STYLE. DON'T BE A HATER.
POP!
COME IN... CAPTAIN, WE NEED BACKUP. THE SECOND HUMMER IS GETTING AWAY.
HEY! LOOK OUT.
KULUDGE
JACK, I'VE LOST THE CAPTAIN'S SIGNAL.
STAY CLOSE ROSE.
OKAY. SOMETHING'S DEFINITELY NOT RIGHT.

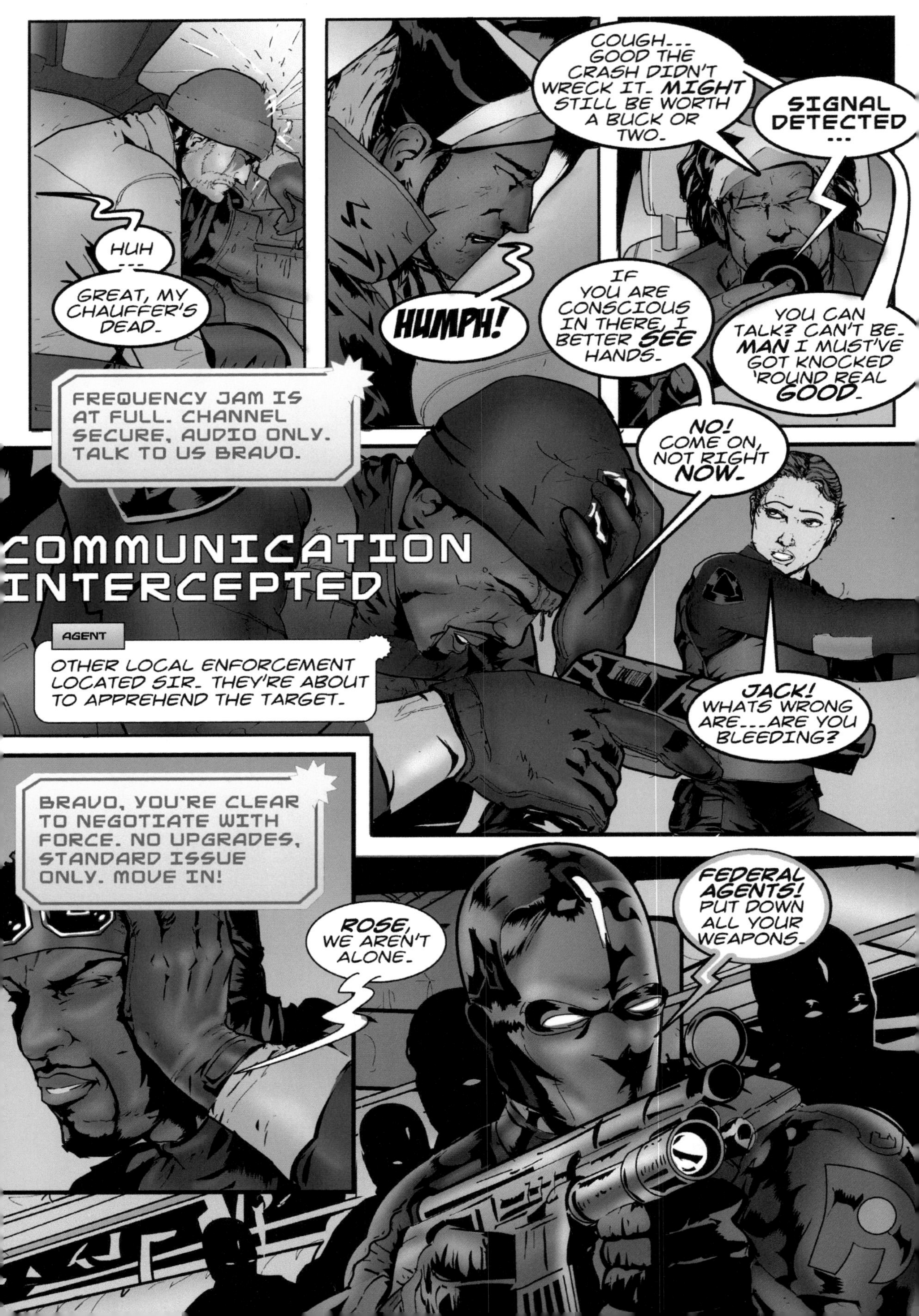
HUH...
GREAT, MY CHAUFFER'S DEAD.
HUMPH!
COUGH... GOOD THE CRASH DIDN'T WRECK IT. MIGHT STILL BE WORTH A BUCK OR TWO.
SIGNAL DETECTED...
IF YOU ARE CONSCIOUS IN THERE, I BETTER SEE HANDS.
YOU CAN TALK? CAN'T BE. MAN I MUST'VE GOT KNOCKED 'ROUND REAL GOOD.
FREQUENCY JAM IS AT FULL. CHANNEL SECURE, AUDIO ONLY. TALK TO US BRAVO.
NO! COME ON, NOT RIGHT NOW.
COMMUNICATION INTERCEPTED
AGENT
OTHER LOCAL ENFORCEMENT LOCATED SIR. THEY'RE ABOUT TO APPREHEND THE TARGET.
JACK! WHATS WRONG ARE...ARE YOU BLEEDING?
BRAVO, YOU'RE CLEAR TO NEGOTIATE WITH FORCE. NO UPGRADES, STANDARD ISSUE ONLY. MOVE IN!
ROSE, WE AREN'T ALONE.
FEDERAL AGENTS! PUT DOWN ALL YOUR WEAPONS.

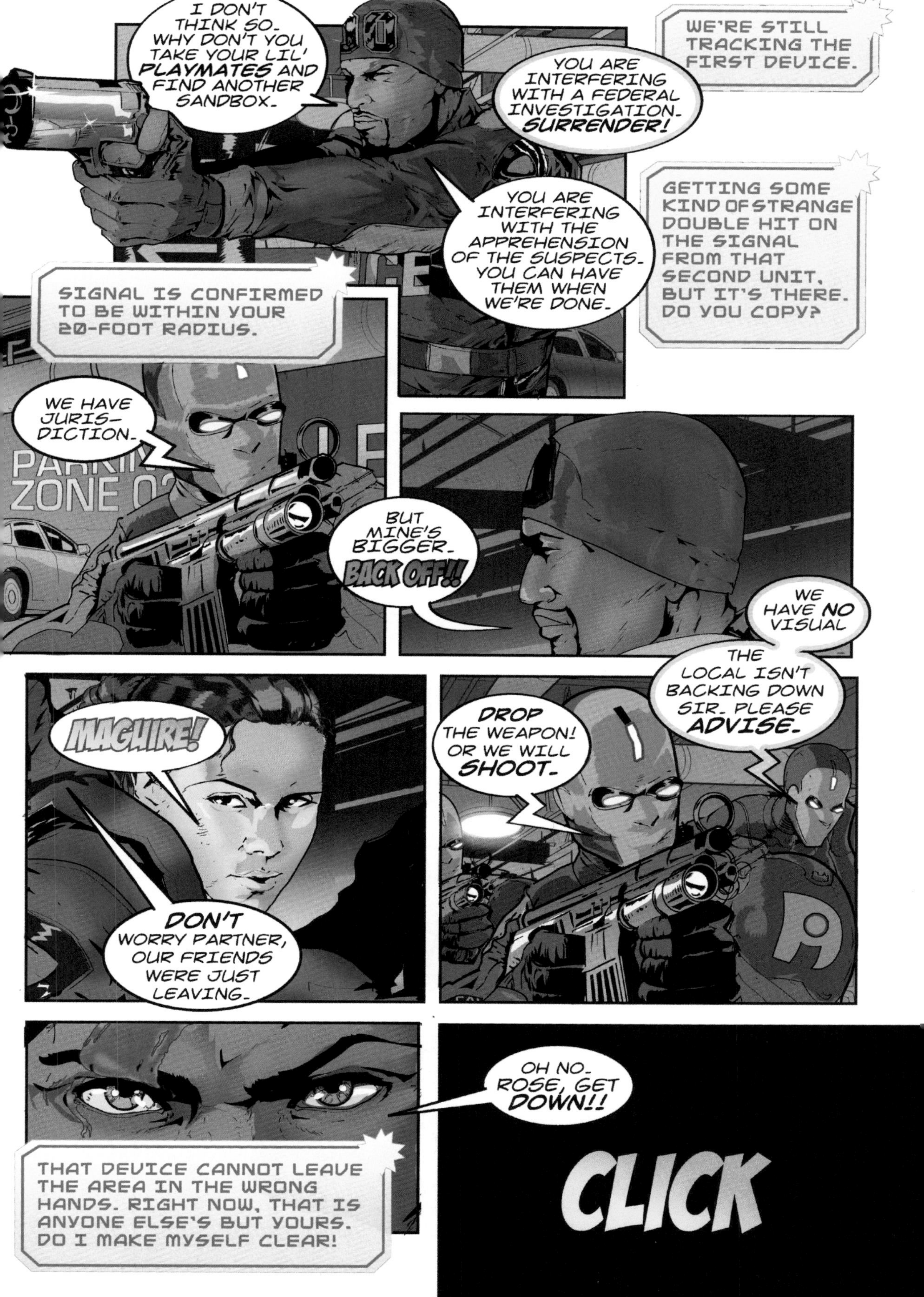
I DON'T THINK SO. WHY DON'T YOU TAKE YOUR LIL' PLAYMATES AND FIND ANOTHER SANDBOX.
YOU ARE INTERFERING WITH A FEDERAL INVESTIGATION. SURRENDER!
WE'RE STILL TRACKING THE FIRST DEVICE.
YOU ARE INTERFERING WITH THE APPREHENSION OF THE SUSPECTS. YOU CAN HAVE THEM WHEN WE'RE DONE.
GETTING SOME KIND OF STRANGE DOUBLE HIT ON THE SIGNAL FROM THAT SECOND UNIT, BUT IT'S THERE. DO YOU COPY?
SIGNAL IS CONFIRMED TO BE WITHIN YOUR 20-FOOT RADIUS.
WE HAVE JURIS-DICTION.
PARKIN ZONE 02
BUT MINE'S BIGGER. BACK OFF!!
WE HAVE NO VISUAL
THE LOCAL ISN'T BACKING DOWN SIR. PLEASE ADVISE.
MAGUIRE!
DON'T WORRY PARTNER, OUR FRIENDS WERE JUST LEAVING.
DROP THE WEAPON! OR WE WILL SHOOT.
OH NO. ROSE, GET DOWN!!
THAT DEVICE CANNOT LEAVE THE AREA IN THE WRONG HANDS. RIGHT NOW, THAT IS ANYONE ELSE'S BUT YOURS. DO I MAKE MYSELF CLEAR!
CLICK

TRAINING LOGS — CLASSIFIED

ENTRY 356 | BASIC DEFENSIVE DRILLS PART 1

BASIC DEFENSIVE EXERCISES WORK IN COMBINATION WITH BOTH BASIC AND ADVANCED COMBAT TRAINING.
SEE ENTRY 798 PARTS 1-300 AND ENTRY 799 PARTS 1-170

EXERCISES

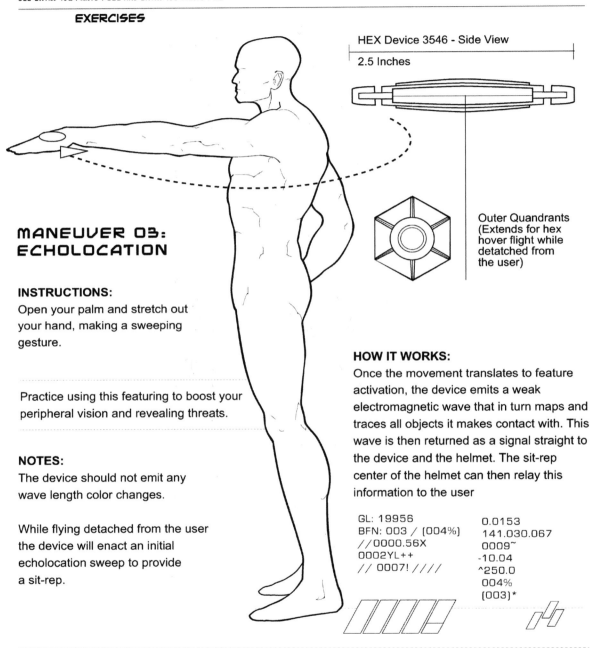

HEX Device 3546 - Side View

2.5 Inches

Outer Quandrants
(Extends for hex
hover flight while
detatched from
the user)

MANEUVER 03: ECHOLOCATION

INSTRUCTIONS:
Open your palm and stretch out
your hand, making a sweeping
gesture.

Practice using this featuring to boost your
peripheral vision and revealing threats.

NOTES:
The device should not emit any
wave length color changes.

While flying detached from the user
the device will enact an initial
echolocation sweep to provide
a sit-rep.

HOW IT WORKS:
Once the movement translates to feature
activation, the device emits a weak
electromagnetic wave that in turn maps and
traces all objects it makes contact with. This
wave is then returned as a signal straight to
the device and the helmet. The sit-rep
center of the helmet can then relay this
information to the user

GL: 19956
BFN: 003 / (004%)
//0000.56X
0002YL++
// 0007! ////

0.0153
141.030.067
0009~
-10.04
^250.0
004%
(003)*

The device will execute echolocation protocol effectively as long as the user's motions are decisive.
In sleep mode the device will not execute echolocation.

SPECS: (This protocol burns no battery life in active mode.)

ENTRY 356 | BASIC DEFENSIVE DRILLS PART 1

BASIC DEFENSIVE EXERCISES WORK IN COMBINATION WITH BOTH BASIC AND ADVANCED COMBAT TRAINING.
SEE ENTRY 798 PARTS 1-300 AND ENTRY 799 PARTS 1-170

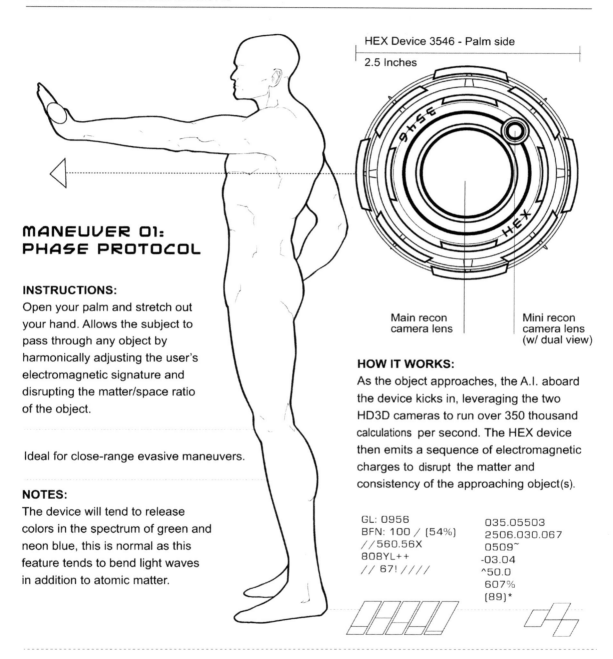

HEX Device 3546 - Palm side

2.5 Inches

MANEUVER 01: PHASE PROTOCOL

INSTRUCTIONS:
Open your palm and stretch out your hand. Allows the subject to pass through any object by harmonically adjusting the user's electromagnetic signature and disrupting the matter/space ratio of the object.

Ideal for close-range evasive maneuvers.

NOTES:
The device will tend to release colors in the spectrum of green and neon blue, this is normal as this feature tends to bend light waves in addition to atomic matter.

Main recon camera lens

Mini recon camera lens (w/ dual view)

HOW IT WORKS:
As the object approaches, the A.I. aboard the device kicks in, leveraging the two HD3D cameras to run over 350 thousand calculations per second. The HEX device then emits a sequence of electromagnetic charges to disrupt the matter and consistency of the approaching object(s).

GL: 0956
BFN: 100 / (54%)
//560.56X
808YL++
// 67! ////

035.05503
2506.030.067
0509~
-03.04
^50.0
607%
(89)*

The device will execute phase protocol effectively as long as the user's motions are decisive.
Set to sleep mode for prolonged or unexpected engagement. A.I. will execute as needed.

SPECS: (This protocol burns no battery life in active mode but trace amounts of meter in sleep mode)

TRAINING LOGS CLASSIFIED

ENTRY 356 | BASIC DEFENSIVE DRILLS PART 1

BASIC DEFENSIVE EXERCISES WORK IN COMBINATION WITH BOTH BASIC AND ADVANCED COMBAT TRAINING.
SEE ENTRY 798 PARTS 1-300 AND ENTRY 799 PARTS 1-170

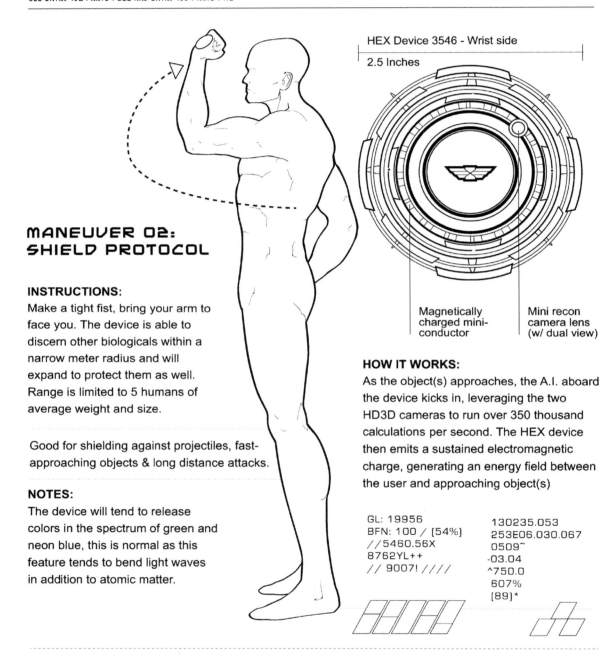

HEX Device 3546 - Wrist side
2.5 Inches
Magnetically charged mini-conductor
Mini recon camera lens (w/ dual view)

MANEUVER 02: SHIELD PROTOCOL

INSTRUCTIONS:
Make a tight fist, bring your arm to face you. The device is able to discern other biologicals within a narrow meter radius and will expand to protect them as well. Range is limited to 5 humans of average weight and size.

Good for shielding against projectiles, fast-approaching objects & long distance attacks.

NOTES:
The device will tend to release colors in the spectrum of green and neon blue, this is normal as this feature tends to bend light waves in addition to atomic matter.

HOW IT WORKS:
As the object(s) approaches, the A.I. aboard the device kicks in, leveraging the two HD3D cameras to run over 350 thousand calculations per second. The HEX device then emits a sustained electromagnetic charge, generating an energy field between the user and approaching object(s)

GL: 19956
BFN: 100 / (54%)
//5460.56X
8762YL++
// 9007! ////

130235.053
253E06.030.067
0509~
-03.04
^750.0
607%
(89)*

The device will execute shield protocol effectively as long as the user's motions are decisive. Set to sleep mode for prolonged or unexpected engagement. A.I. will execute as needed.

SPECS: (This protocol burns no battery life in active mode but trace amounts of meter in sleep mode)

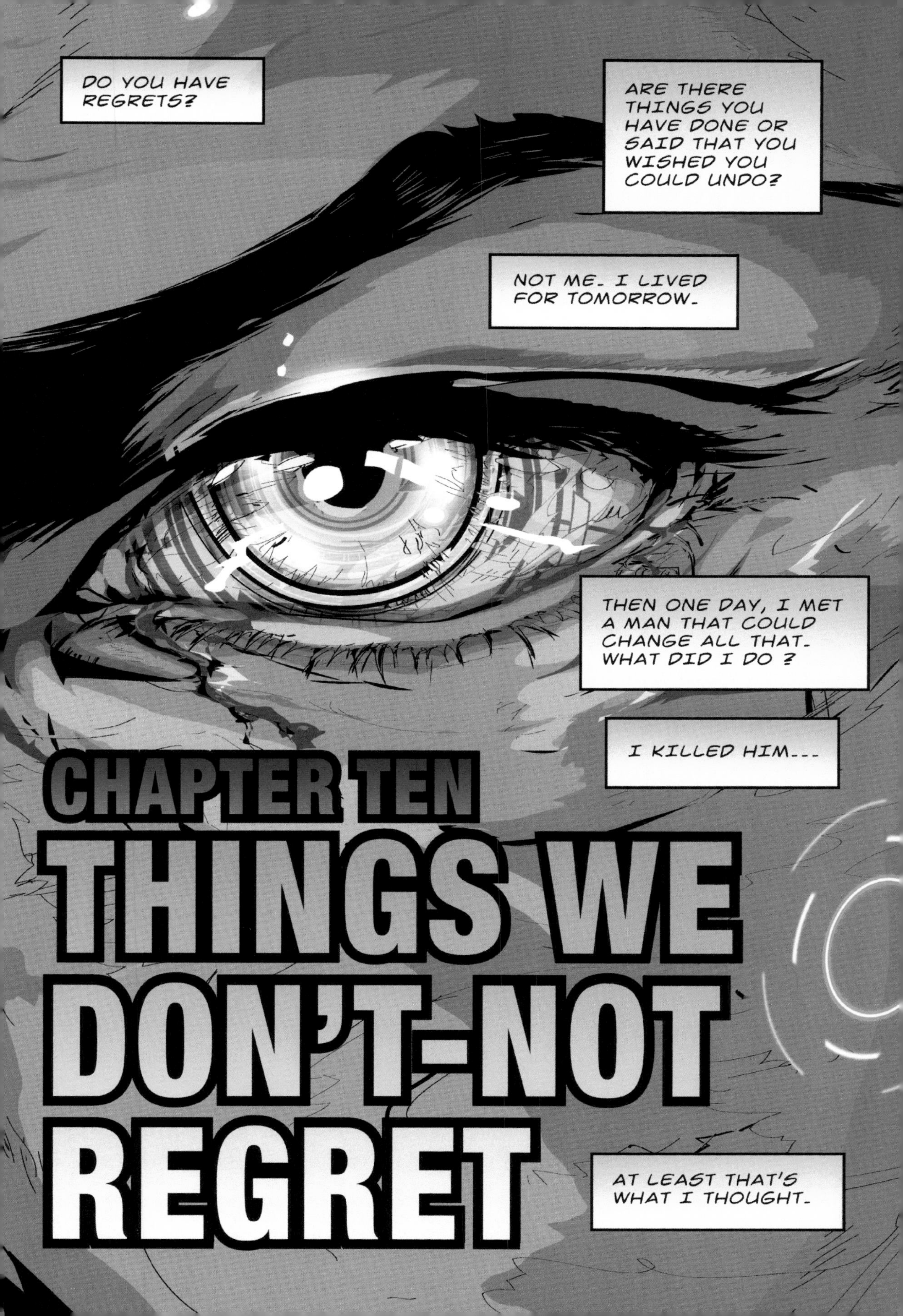
DO YOU HAVE REGRETS?
ARE THERE THINGS YOU HAVE DONE OR SAID THAT YOU WISHED YOU COULD UNDO?
NOT ME. I LIVED FOR TOMORROW.
THEN ONE DAY, I MET A MAN THAT COULD CHANGE ALL THAT. WHAT DID I DO ?
I KILLED HIM...
CHAPTER TEN
THINGS WE DON'T-NOT REGRET
AT LEAST THAT'S WHAT I THOUGHT.

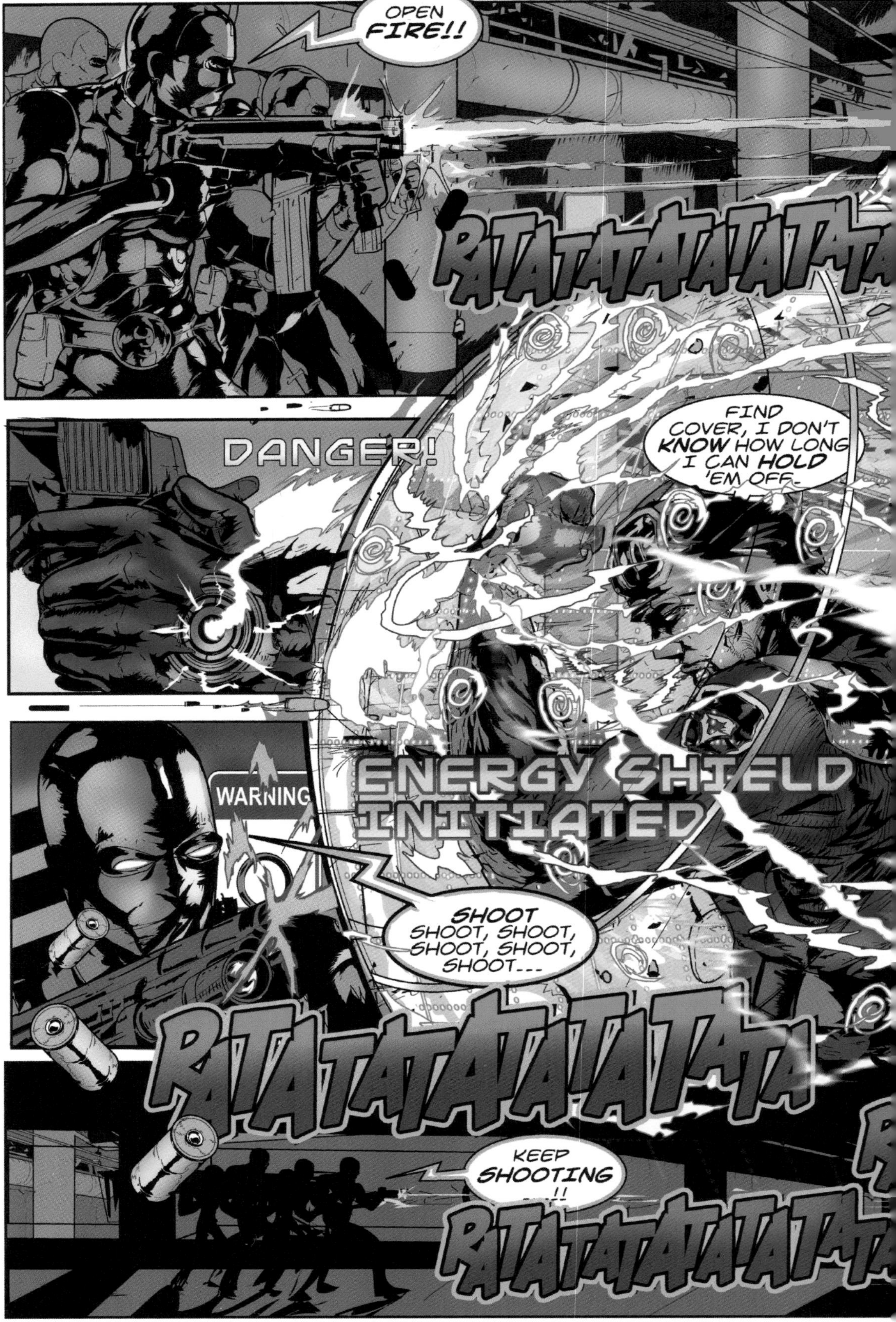
OPEN FIRE!!
RATATATATATATATA
DANGER!
FIND COVER, I DON'T KNOW HOW LONG I CAN HOLD 'EM OFF-
WARNING
ENERGY SHIELD INITIATED
SHOOT SHOOT, SHOOT, SHOOT, SHOOT, SHOOT---
RATATATATATATATA
KEEP SHOOTING --!!
RATATATATATATATA

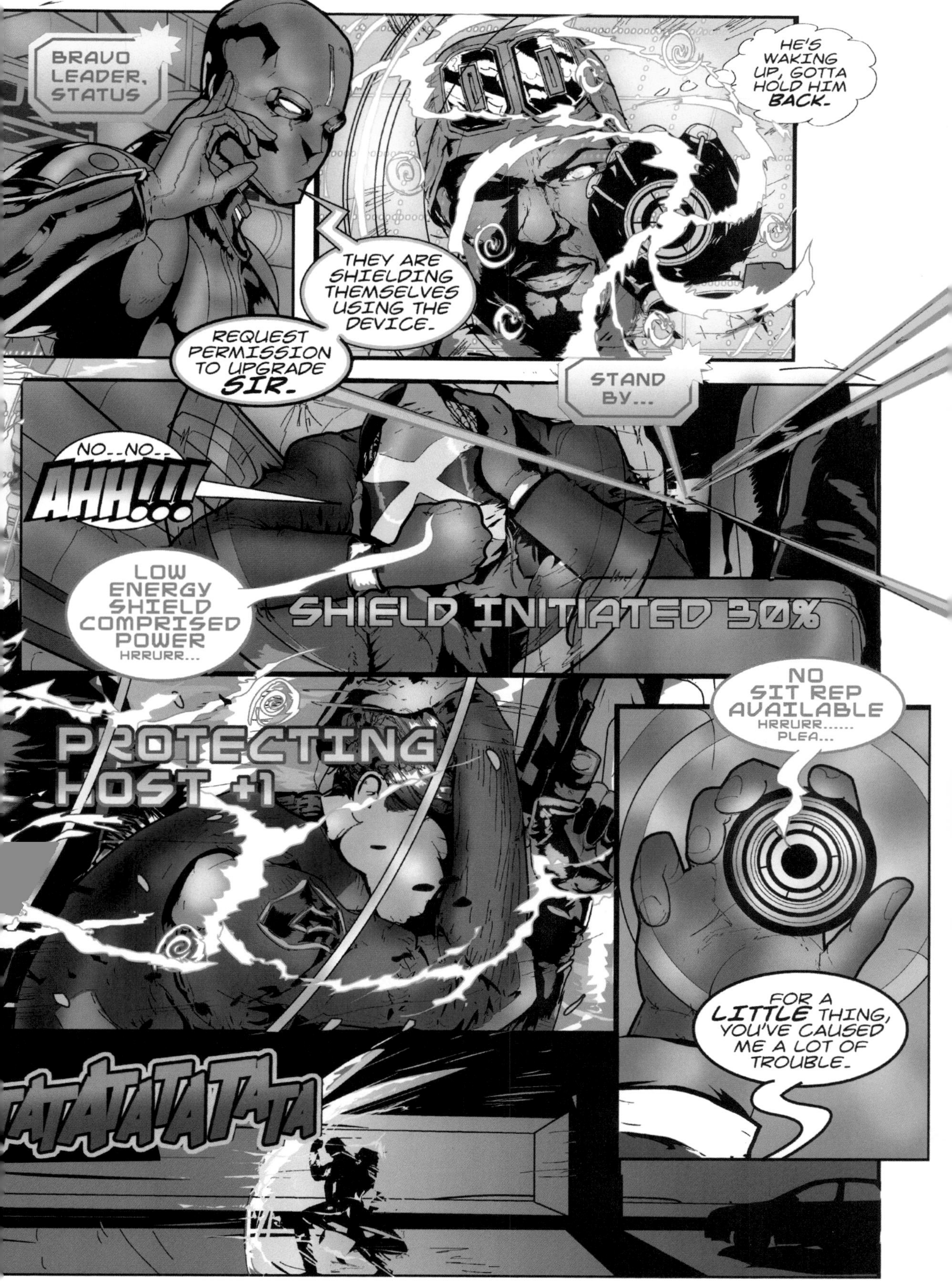
BRAVO LEADER, STATUS
HE'S WAKING UP, GOTTA HOLD HIM BACK.
THEY ARE SHIELDING THEMSELVES USING THE DEVICE.
REQUEST PERMISSION TO UPGRADE SIR.
STAND BY...
NO..NO.. AHH!!!...
LOW ENERGY SHIELD COMPRISED POWER HRRURR...
SHIELD INITIATED 30%
PROTECTING HOST +1
NO SIT REP AVAILABLE HRRURR...... PLEA...
FOR A LITTLE THING, YOU'VE CAUSED ME A LOT OF TROUBLE.
TATATATATATATA

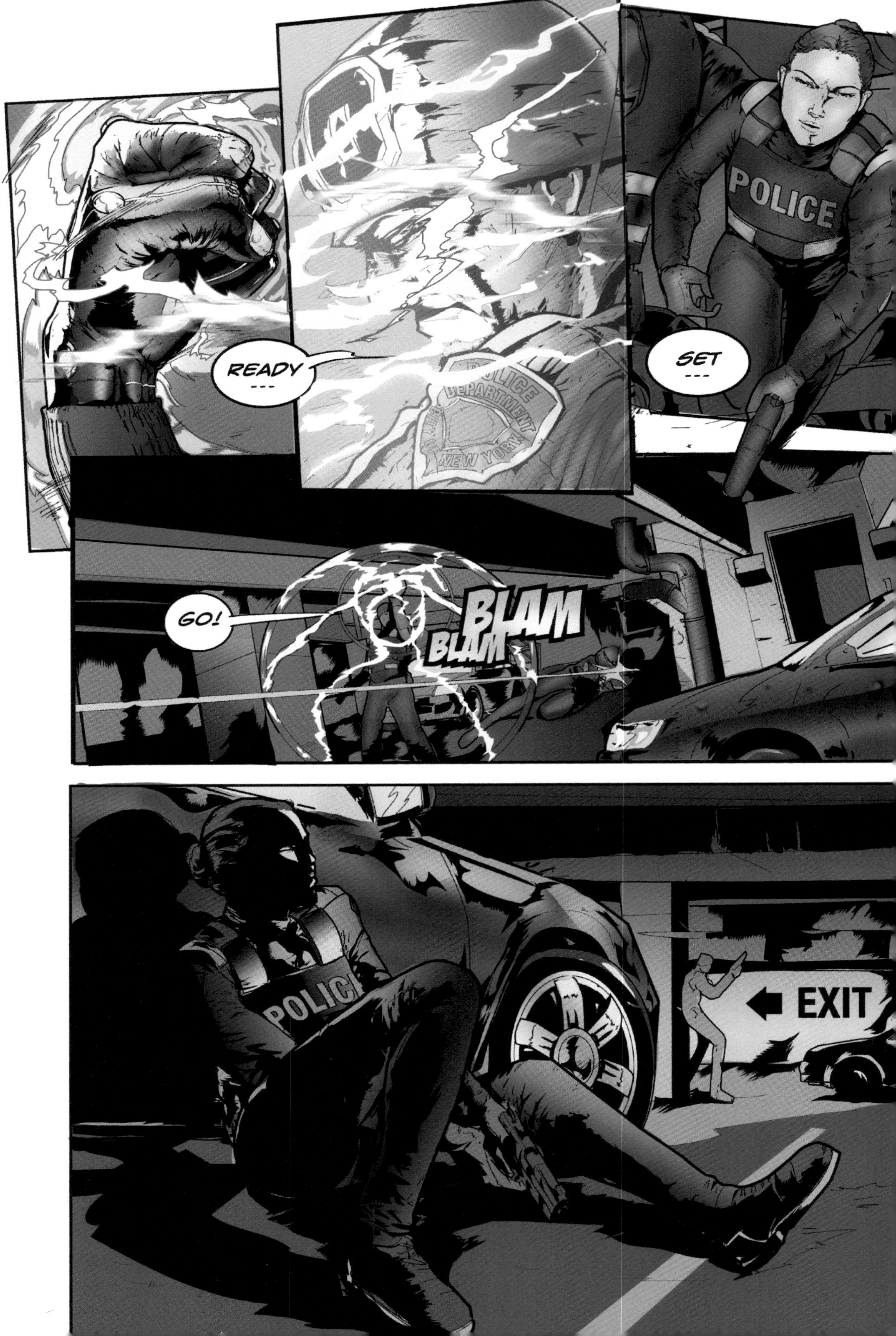
READY ---
SET ---
POLICE
POLICE DEPARTMENT CITY OF NEW YORK
GO!
BLAM
BLAM
POLIC
EXIT

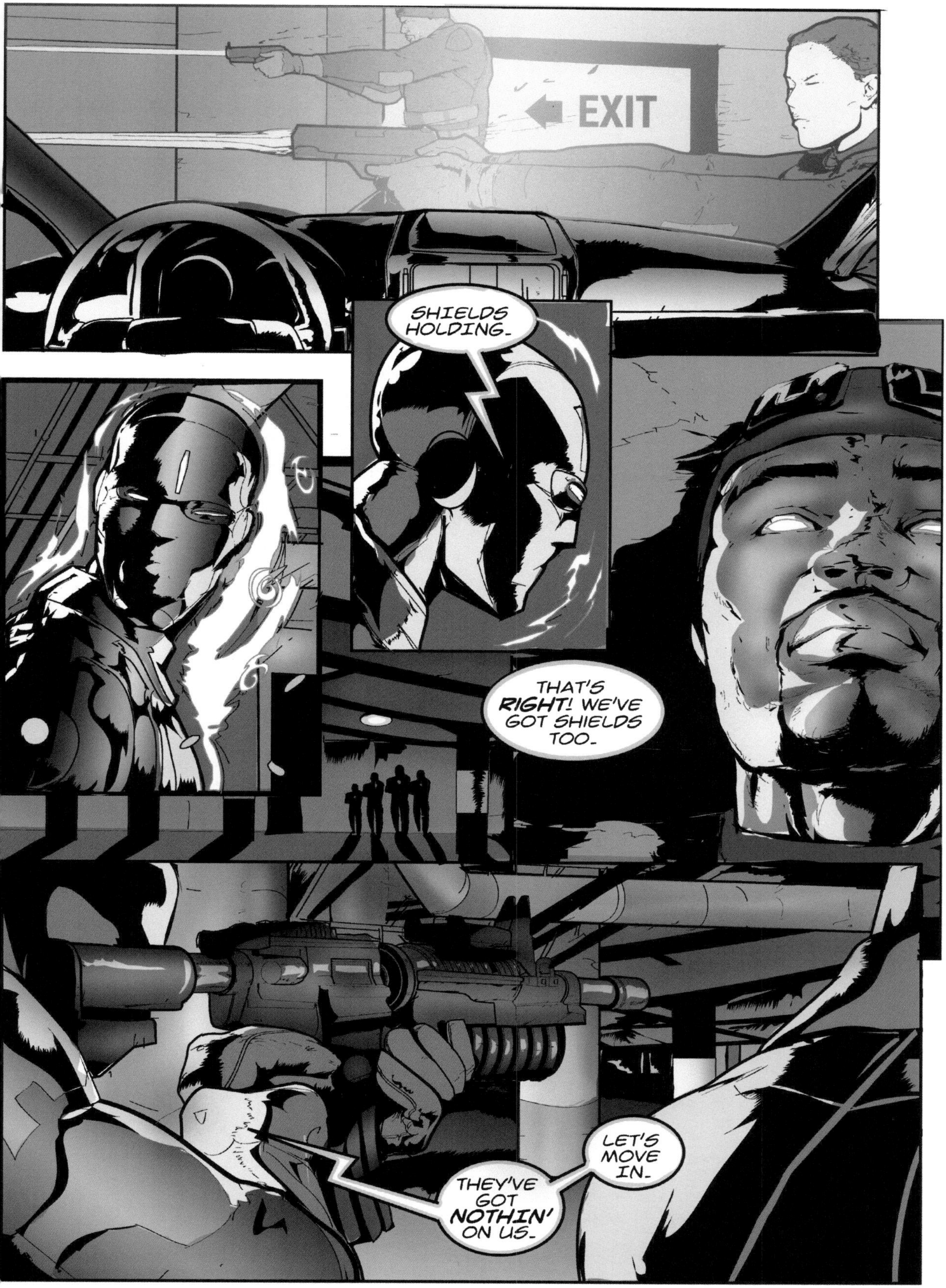
EXIT
SHIELDS HOLDING.
THAT'S RIGHT! WE'VE GOT SHIELDS TOO.
THEY'VE GOT NOTHIN' ON US.
LET'S MOVE IN.

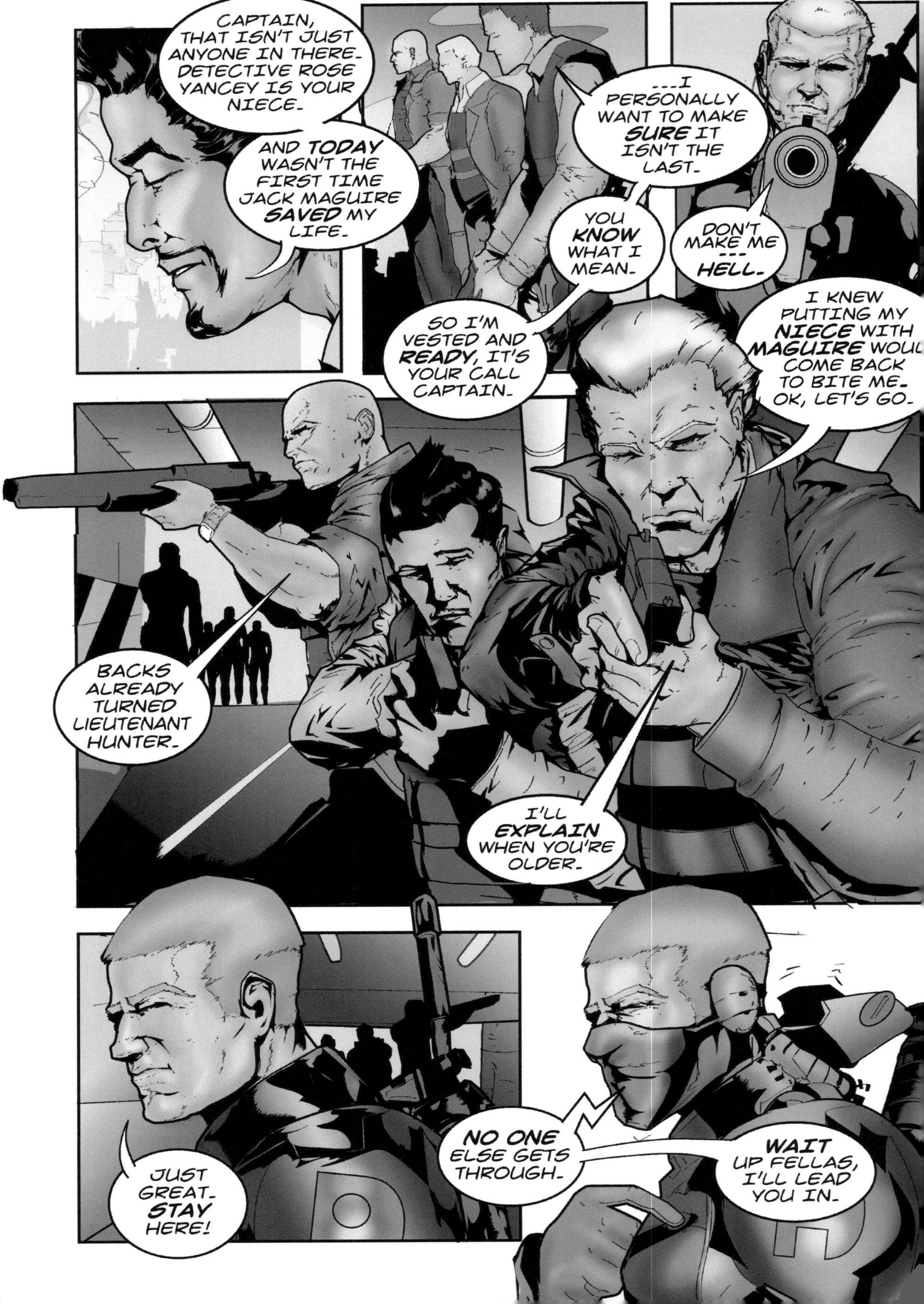
CAPTAIN, THAT ISN'T JUST ANYONE IN THERE. DETECTIVE ROSE YANCEY IS YOUR NIECE.
AND TODAY WASN'T THE FIRST TIME JACK MAGUIRE SAVED MY LIFE.
...I PERSONALLY WANT TO MAKE SURE IT ISN'T THE LAST.
YOU KNOW WHAT I MEAN.
DON'T MAKE ME ... HELL.
SO I'M VESTED AND READY, IT'S YOUR CALL CAPTAIN.
I KNEW PUTTING MY NIECE WITH MAGUIRE WOUL COME BACK TO BITE ME. OK, LET'S GO.
BACKS ALREADY TURNED LIEUTENANT HUNTER.
I'LL EXPLAIN WHEN YOU'RE OLDER.
JUST GREAT. STAY HERE!
NO ONE ELSE GETS THROUGH.
WAIT UP FELLAS, I'LL LEAD YOU IN.

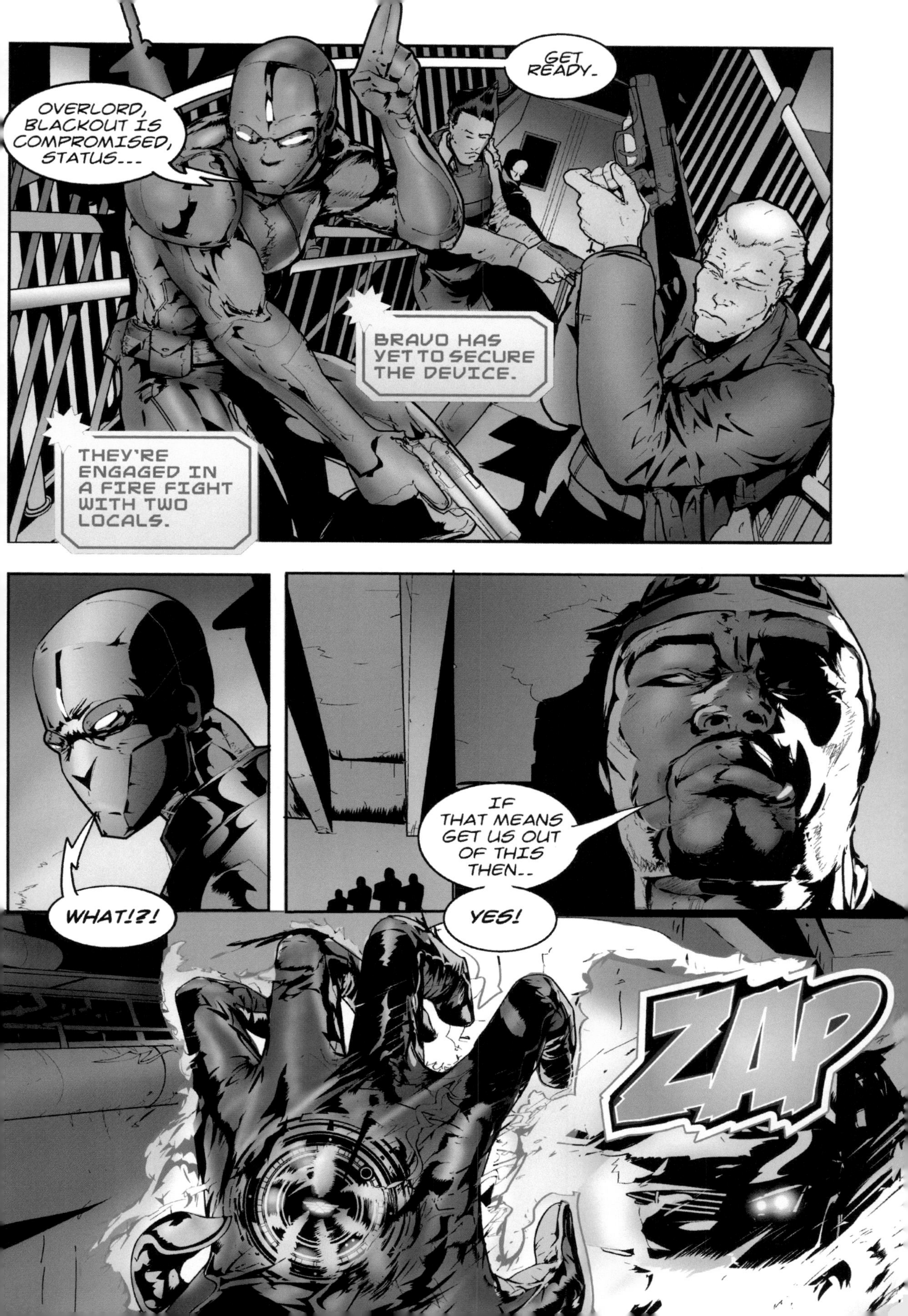
OVERLORD, BLACKOUT IS COMPROMISED, STATUS...
GET READY.
BRAVO HAS YET TO SECURE THE DEVICE.
THEY'RE ENGAGED IN A FIRE FIGHT WITH TWO LOCALS.
WHAT!?!
IF THAT MEANS GET US OUT OF THIS THEN..
YES!
ZAP

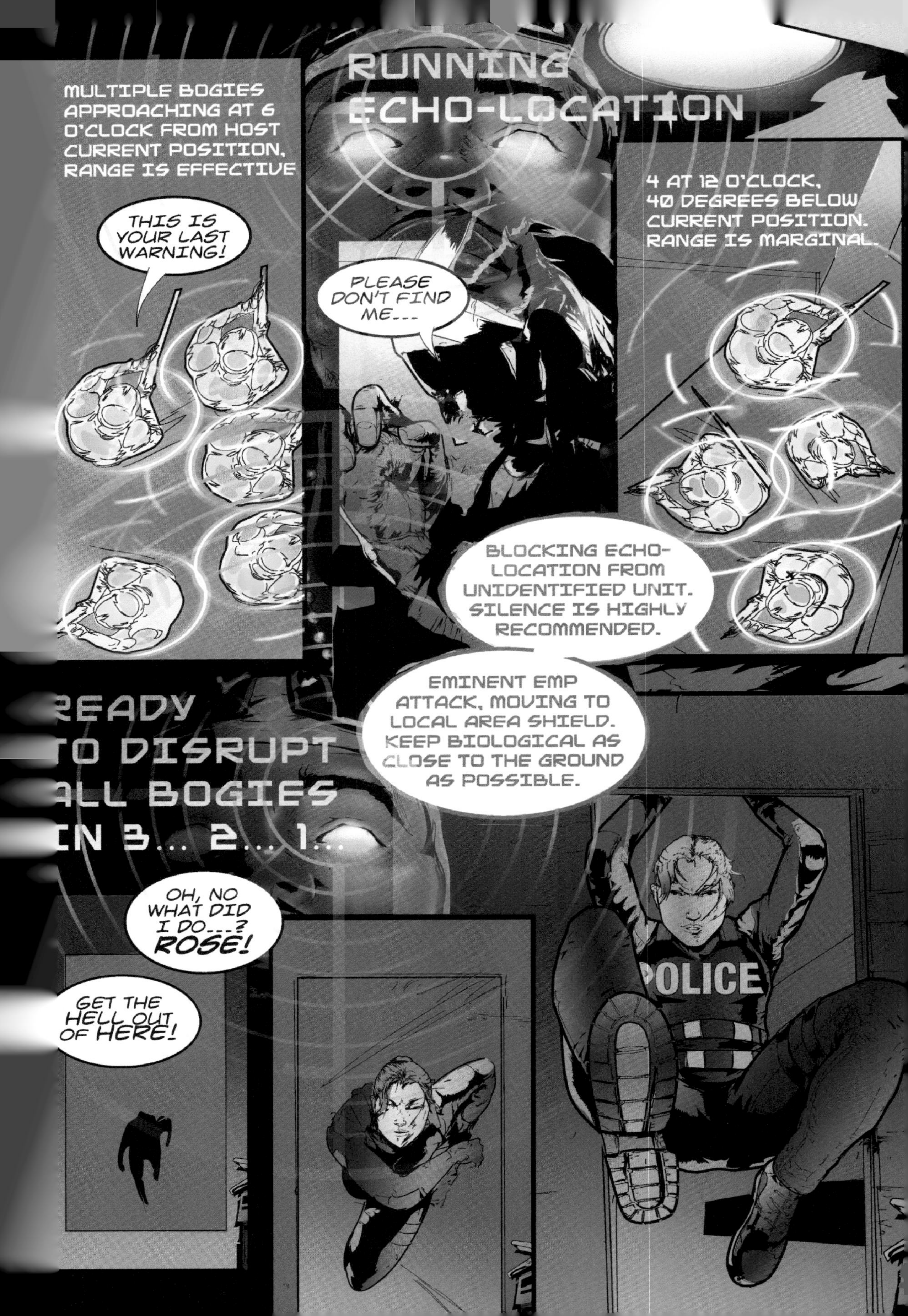
RUNNING ECHO-LOCATION
MULTIPLE BOGIES APPROACHING AT 6 O'CLOCK FROM HOST CURRENT POSITION, RANGE IS EFFECTIVE
THIS IS YOUR LAST WARNING!
PLEASE DON'T FIND ME...
4 AT 12 O'CLOCK, 40 DEGREES BELOW CURRENT POSITION. RANGE IS MARGINAL.
BLOCKING ECHO-LOCATION FROM UNIDENTIFIED UNIT. SILENCE IS HIGHLY RECOMMENDED.
EMINENT EMP ATTACK, MOVING TO LOCAL AREA SHIELD. KEEP BIOLOGICAL AS CLOSE TO THE GROUND AS POSSIBLE.
READY TO DISRUPT ALL BOGIES IN 3... 2... 1...
OH, NO WHAT DID I DO...? ROSE!
GET THE HELL OUT OF HERE!
POLICE

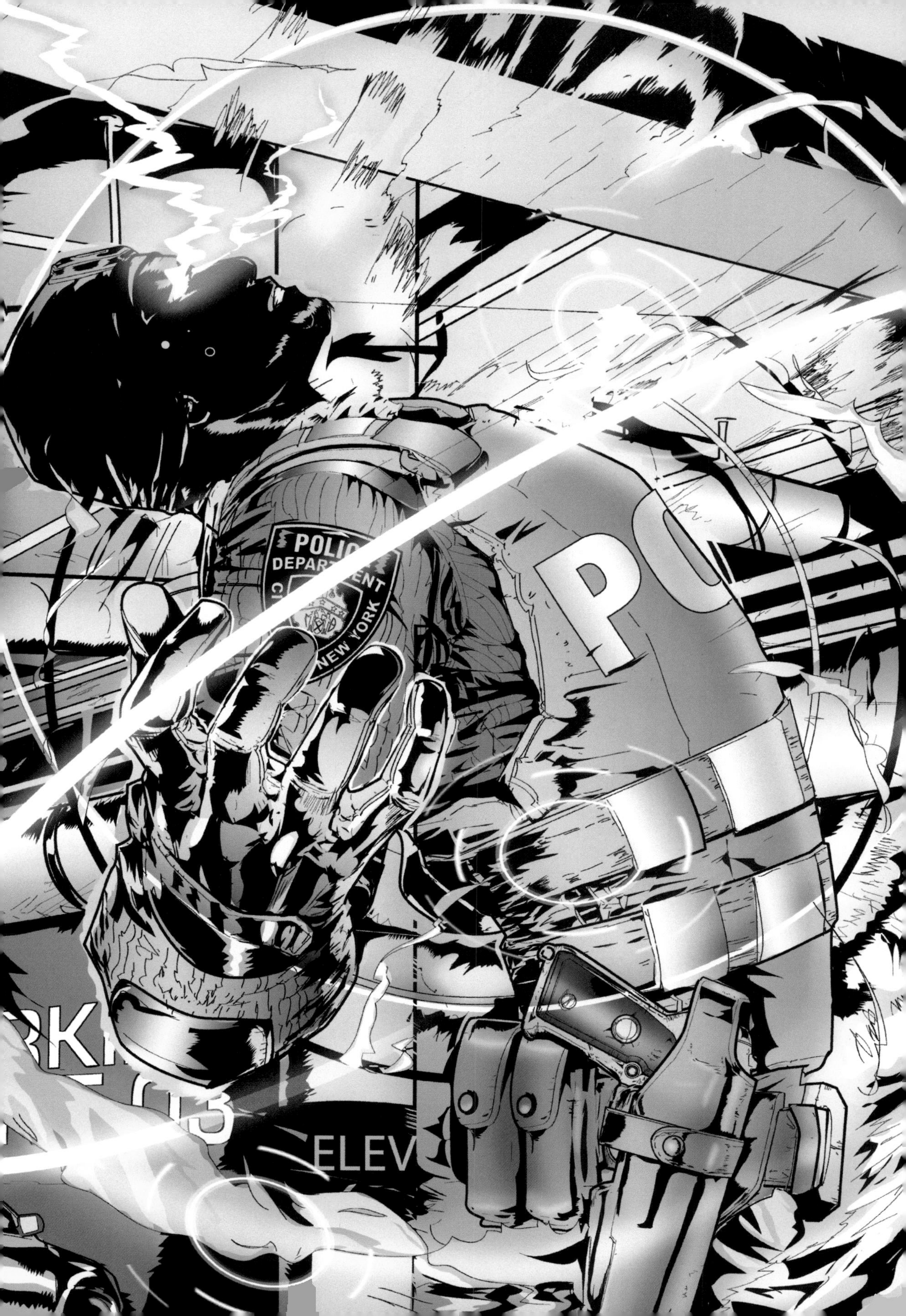
POLIC
DEPART
NEW YORK
P
ELEV

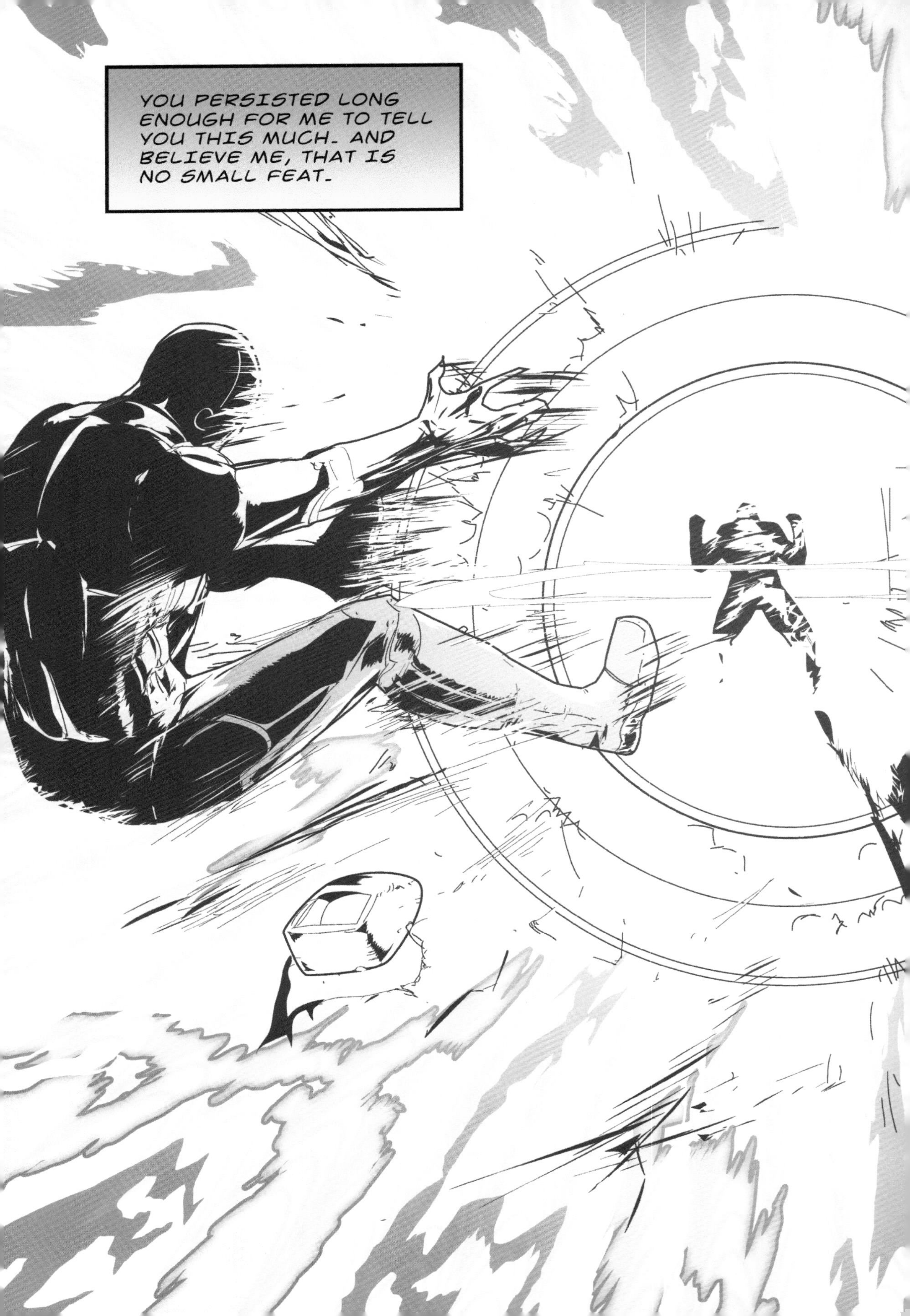
YOU PERSISTED LONG ENOUGH FOR ME TO TELL YOU THIS MUCH. AND BELIEVE ME, THAT IS NO SMALL FEAT.

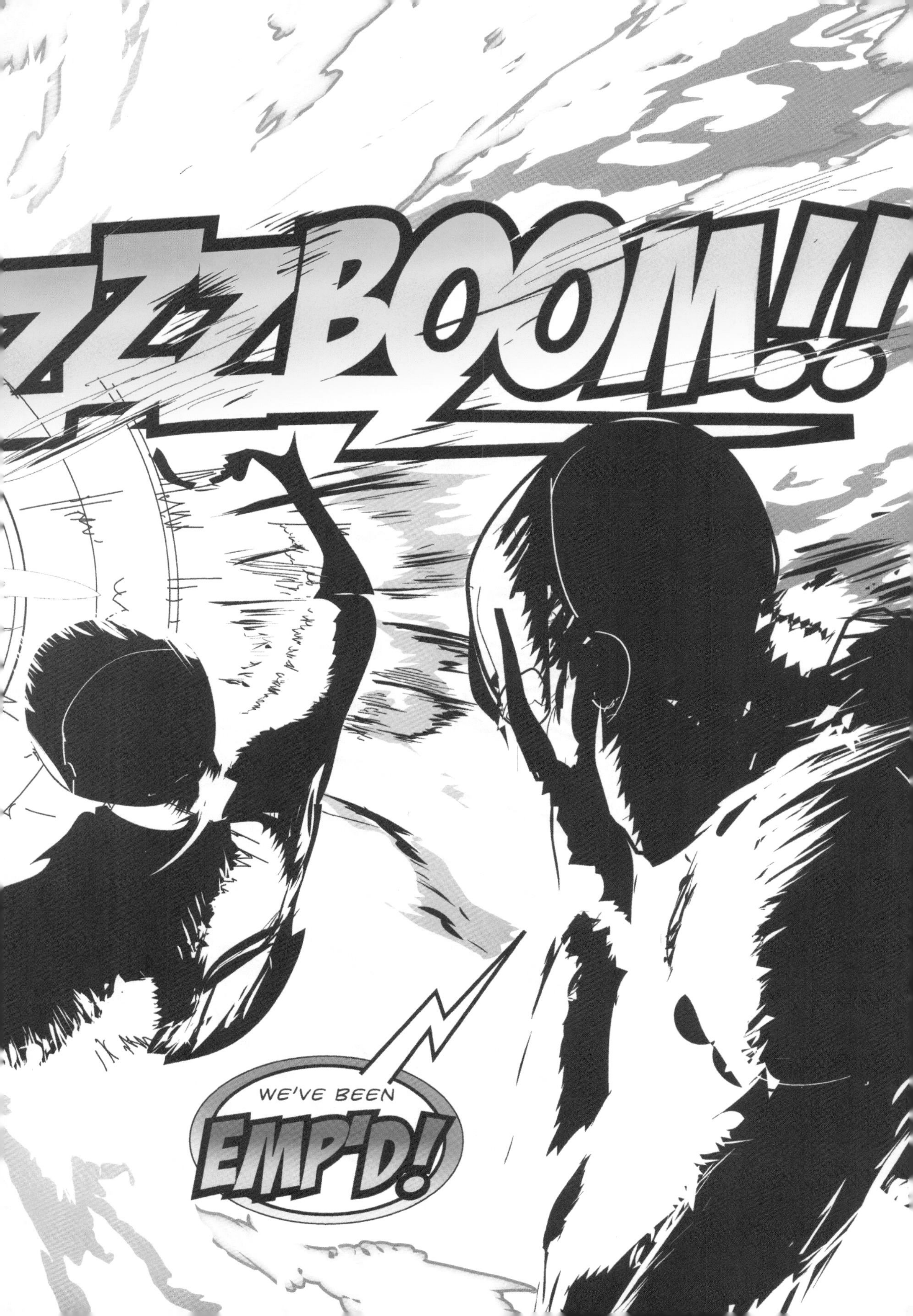
ZZBOOM!!
WE'VE BEEN
EMP'D!

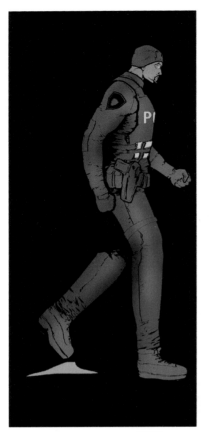

THE INITIAL OUTCOME WAS UNEXPECTED,

NEVERTHELESS I MUST REMAIN UNATTACHED.

SHOW NO INDECISION OR DOUBLE-MINDEDNESS.

FOR A BRIDGE IS NEVER THE FINAL DESTI-NATION.

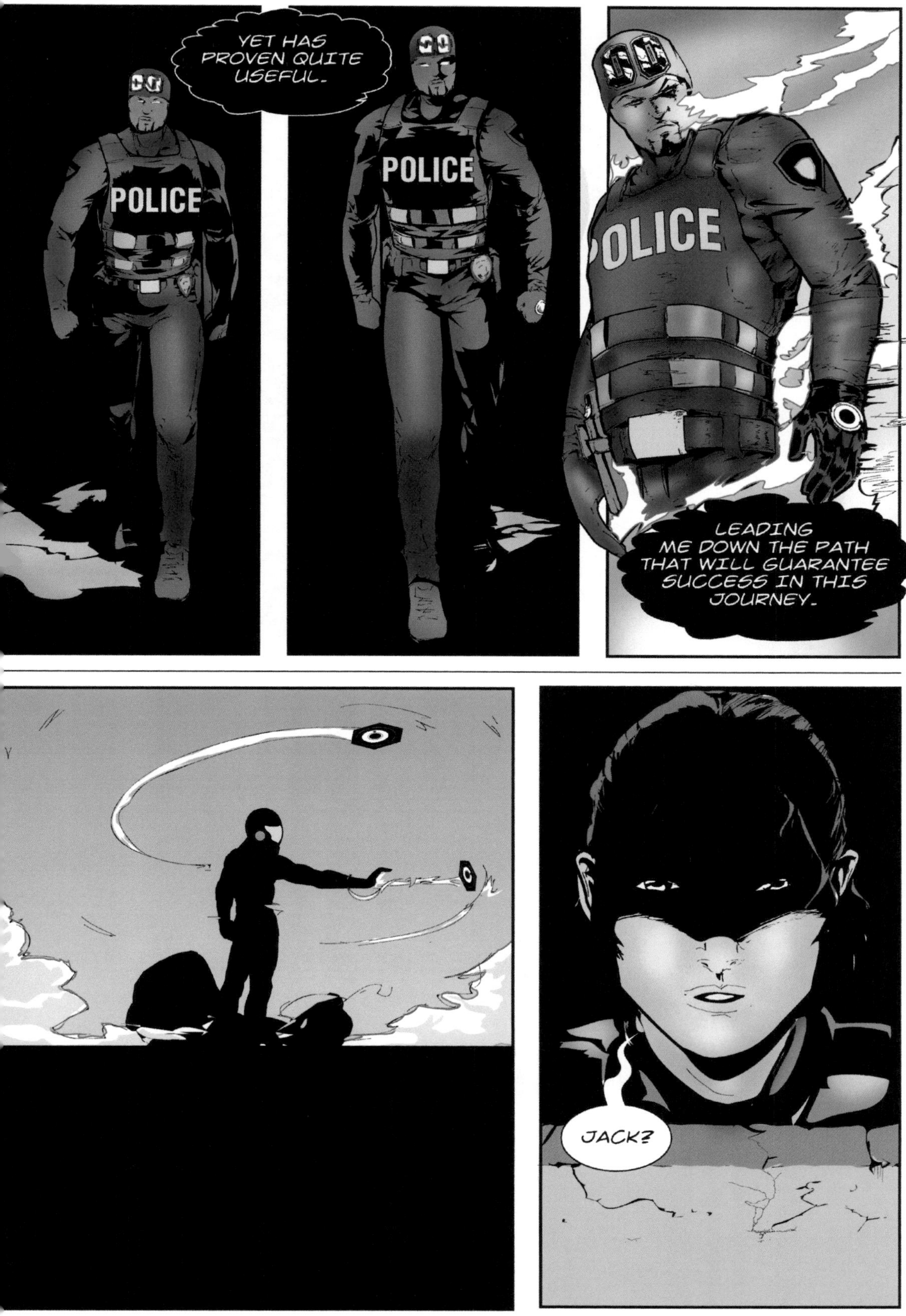
POLICE
YET HAS PROVEN QUITE USEFUL.
POLICE
POLICE
LEADING ME DOWN THE PATH THAT WILL GUARANTEE SUCCESS IN THIS JOURNEY.
JACK?

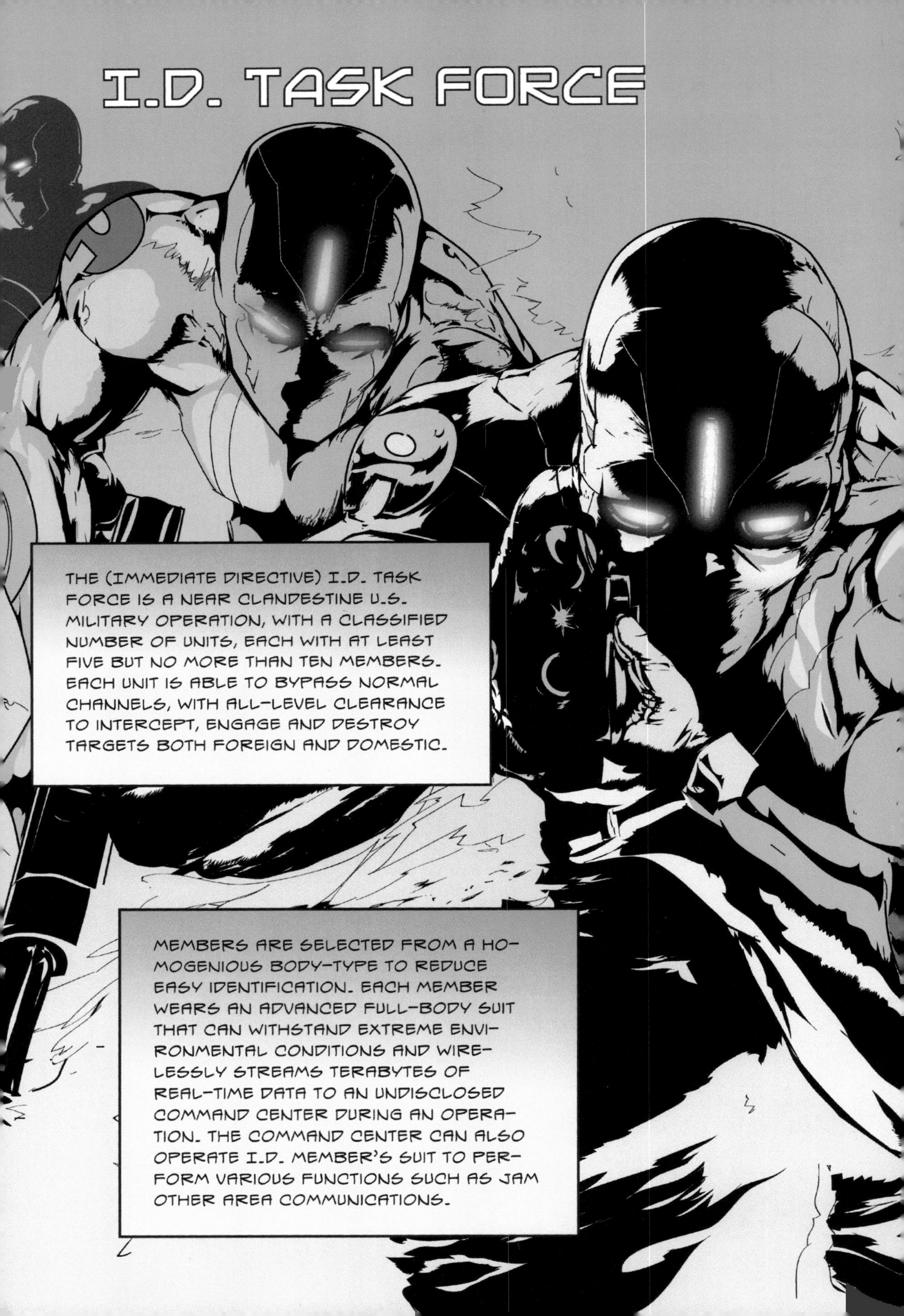
I.D. TASK FORCE
THE (IMMEDIATE DIRECTIVE) I.D. TASK FORCE IS A NEAR CLANDESTINE U.S. MILITARY OPERATION, WITH A CLASSIFIED NUMBER OF UNITS, EACH WITH AT LEAST FIVE BUT NO MORE THAN TEN MEMBERS. EACH UNIT IS ABLE TO BYPASS NORMAL CHANNELS, WITH ALL-LEVEL CLEARANCE TO INTERCEPT, ENGAGE AND DESTROY TARGETS BOTH FOREIGN AND DOMESTIC.
MEMBERS ARE SELECTED FROM A HOMOGENIOUS BODY-TYPE TO REDUCE EASY IDENTIFICATION. EACH MEMBER WEARS AN ADVANCED FULL-BODY SUIT THAT CAN WITHSTAND EXTREME ENVIRONMENTAL CONDITIONS AND WIRELESSLY STREAMS TERABYTES OF REAL-TIME DATA TO AN UNDISCLOSED COMMAND CENTER DURING AN OPERATION. THE COMMAND CENTER CAN ALSO OPERATE I.D. MEMBER'S SUIT TO PERFORM VARIOUS FUNCTIONS SUCH AS JAM OTHER AREA COMMUNICATIONS.

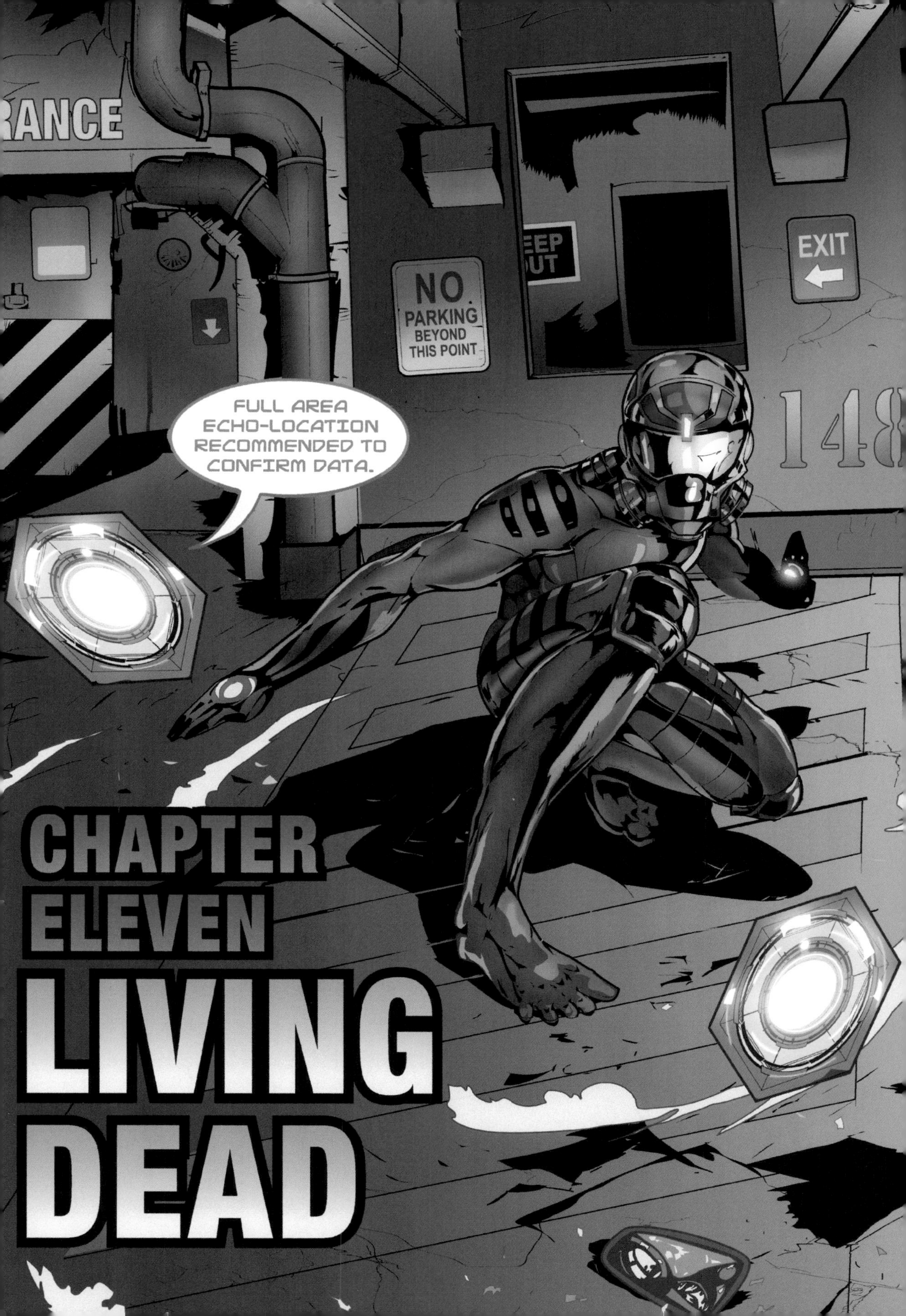
RANCE
NO PARKING BEYOND THIS POINT
EEP OUT
EXIT
148
FULL AREA ECHO-LOCATION RECOMMENDED TO CONFIRM DATA.
CHAPTER ELEVEN
LIVING DEAD

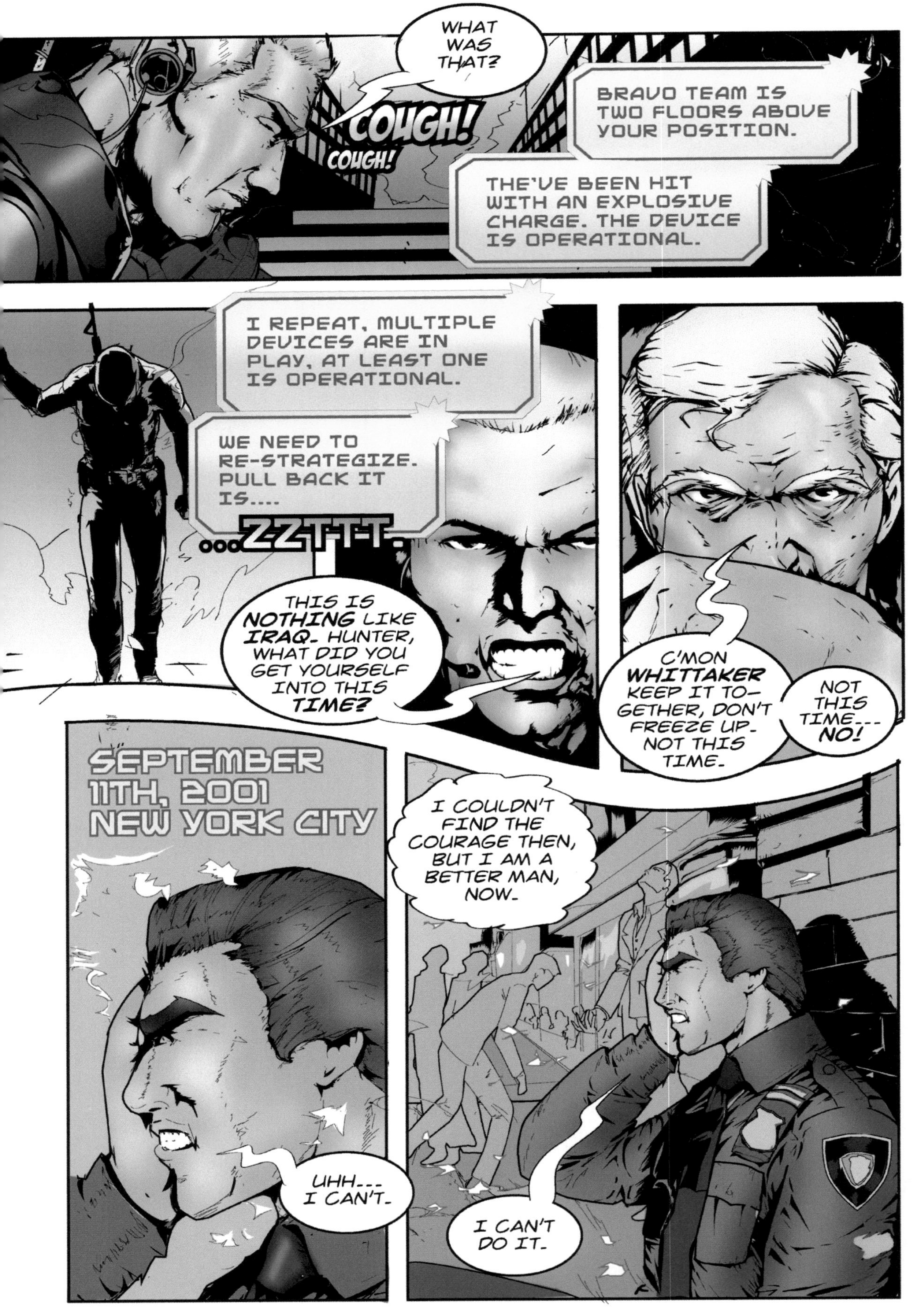
WHAT WAS THAT?
COUGH!
COUGH!
BRAVO TEAM IS TWO FLOORS ABOVE YOUR POSITION.
THE'VE BEEN HIT WITH AN EXPLOSIVE CHARGE. THE DEVICE IS OPERATIONAL.
I REPEAT, MULTIPLE DEVICES ARE IN PLAY, AT LEAST ONE IS OPERATIONAL.
WE NEED TO RE-STRATEGIZE. PULL BACK IT IS....
...ZZTTT.
THIS IS NOTHING LIKE IRAQ. HUNTER, WHAT DID YOU GET YOURSELF INTO THIS TIME?
C'MON WHITTAKER KEEP IT TO-GETHER, DON'T FREEZE UP. NOT THIS TIME.
NOT THIS TIME... NO!
SEPTEMBER 11TH, 2001 NEW YORK CITY
UHH... I CAN'T.
I COULDN'T FIND THE COURAGE THEN, BUT I AM A BETTER MAN, NOW.
I CAN'T DO IT.

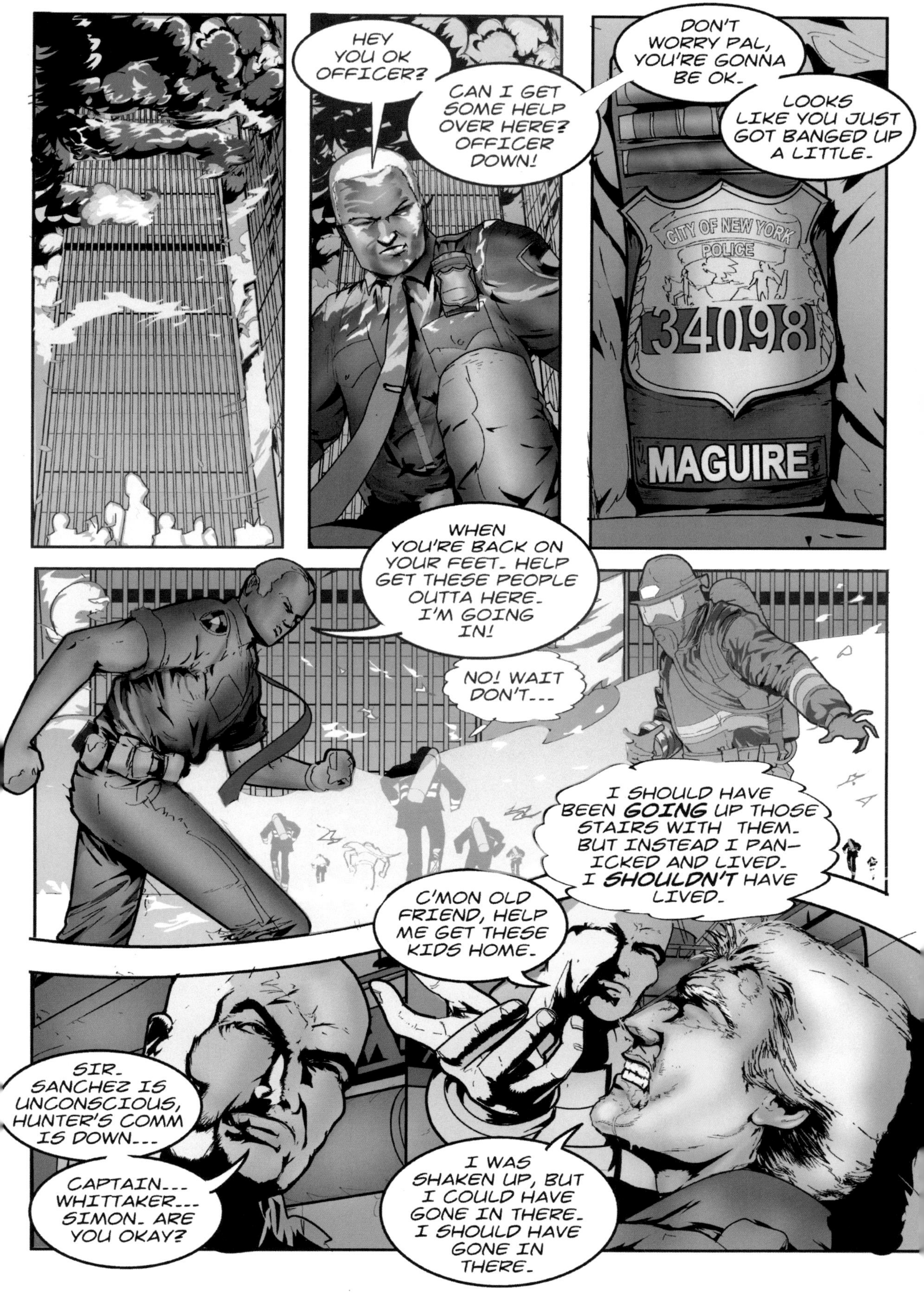
HEY YOU OK OFFICER?
CAN I GET SOME HELP OVER HERE? OFFICER DOWN!
DON'T WORRY PAL, YOU'RE GONNA BE OK.
LOOKS LIKE YOU JUST GOT BANGED UP A LITTLE.
CITY OF NEW YORK
POLICE
34098
MAGUIRE
WHEN YOU'RE BACK ON YOUR FEET. HELP GET THESE PEOPLE OUTTA HERE. I'M GOING IN!
NO! WAIT DON'T...
I SHOULD HAVE BEEN **GOING** UP THOSE STAIRS WITH THEM. BUT INSTEAD I PANICKED AND LIVED. I **SHOULDN'T** HAVE LIVED.
C'MON OLD FRIEND, HELP ME GET THESE KIDS HOME.
SIR. SANCHEZ IS UNCONSCIOUS, HUNTER'S COMM IS DOWN...
CAPTAIN... WHITTAKER... SIMON. ARE YOU OKAY?
I WAS SHAKEN UP, BUT I COULD HAVE GONE IN THERE. I SHOULD HAVE GONE IN THERE.

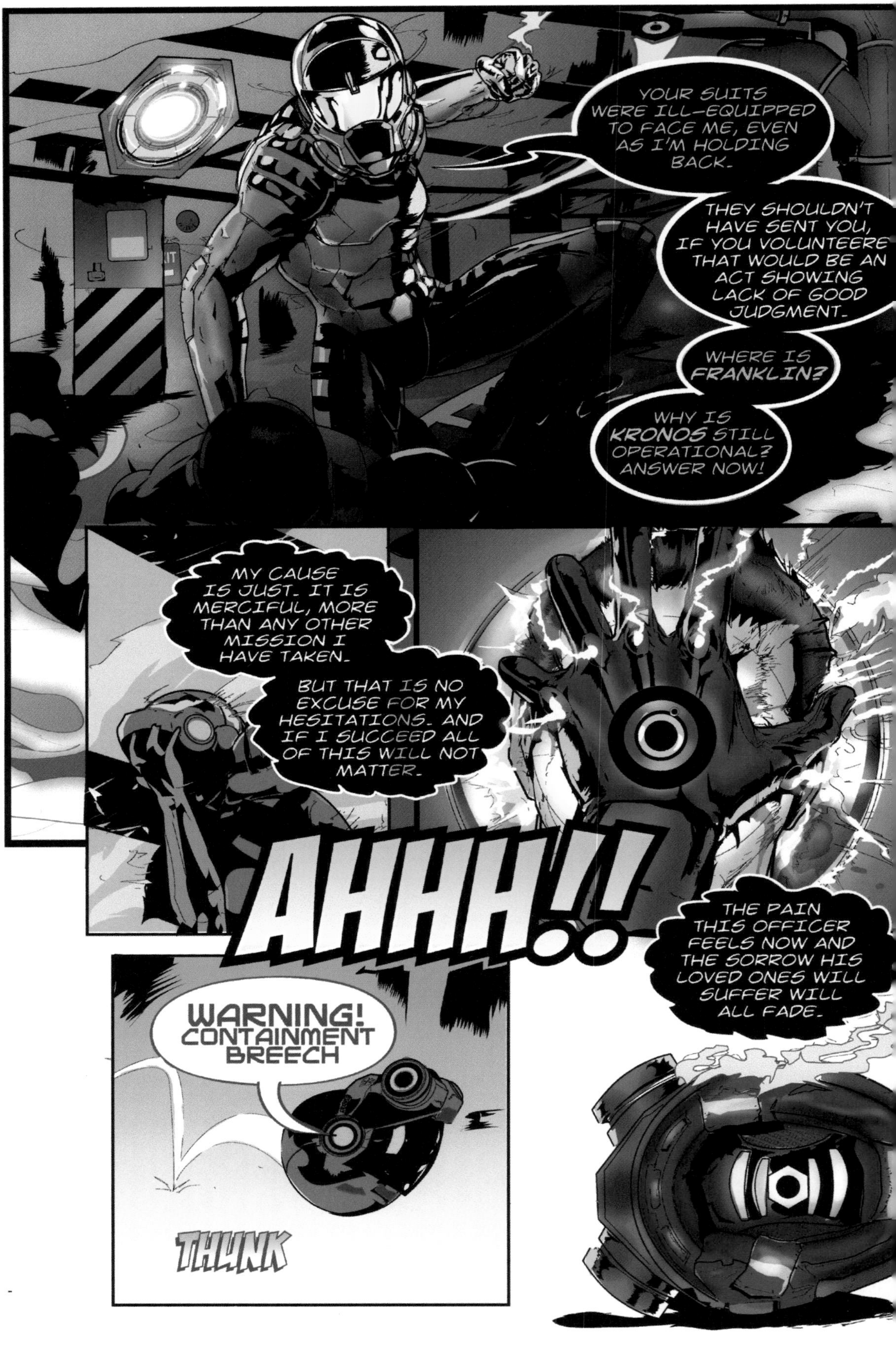
YOUR SUITS WERE ILL-EQUIPPED TO FACE ME, EVEN AS I'M HOLDING BACK.
THEY SHOULDN'T HAVE SENT YOU, IF YOU VOLUNTEERE THAT WOULD BE AN ACT SHOWING LACK OF GOOD JUDGMENT.
WHERE IS FRANKLIN?
WHY IS KRONOS STILL OPERATIONAL? ANSWER NOW!
MY CAUSE IS JUST. IT IS MERCIFUL, MORE THAN ANY OTHER MISSION I HAVE TAKEN.
BUT THAT IS NO EXCUSE FOR MY HESITATIONS. AND IF I SUCCEED ALL OF THIS WILL NOT MATTER.
AHHH!!
THE PAIN THIS OFFICER FEELS NOW AND THE SORROW HIS LOVED ONES WILL SUFFER WILL ALL FADE.
WARNING! CONTAINMENT BREECH
THUNK

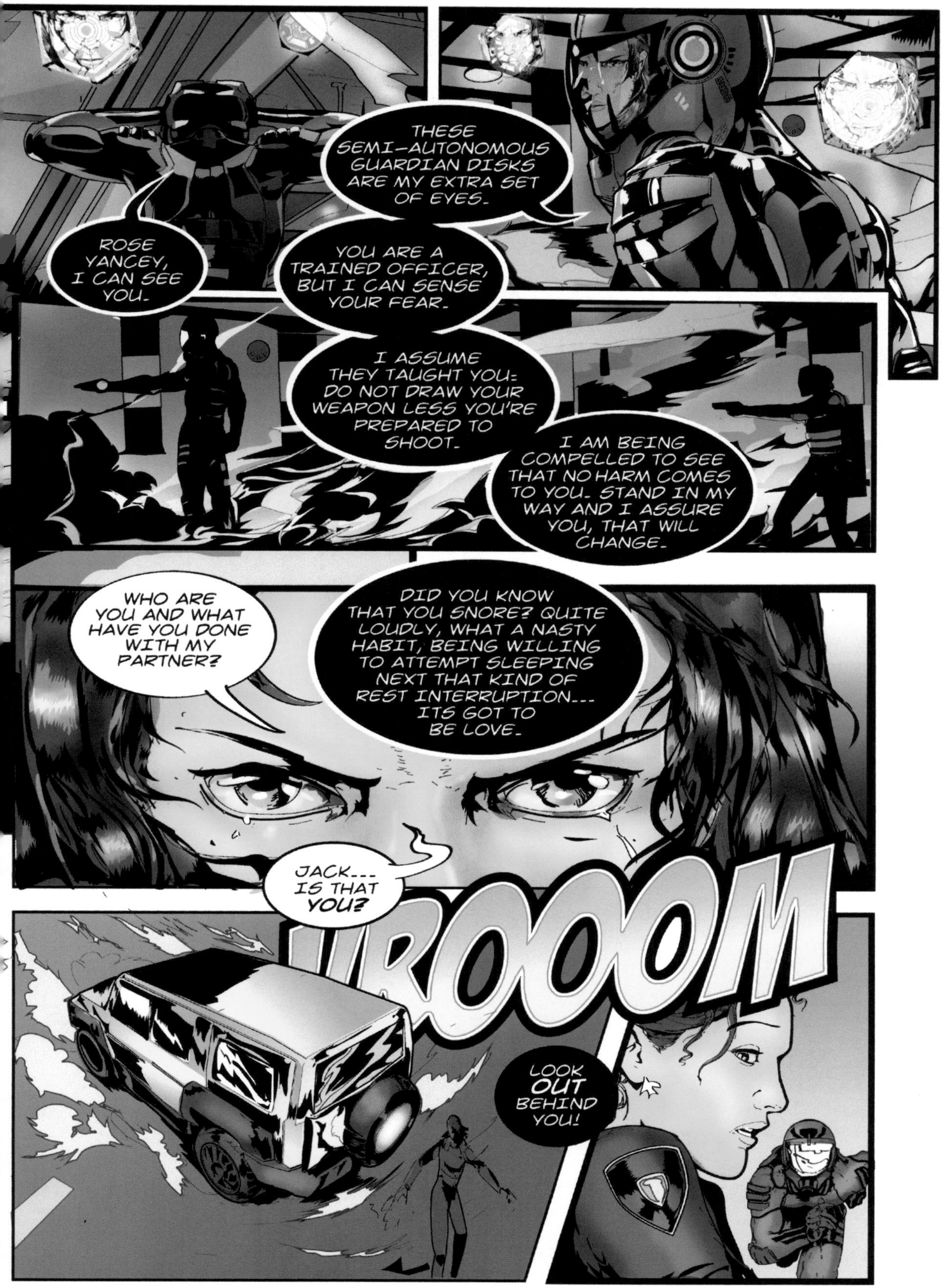
THESE SEMI-AUTONOMOUS GUARDIAN DISKS ARE MY EXTRA SET OF EYES.
ROSE YANCEY, I CAN SEE YOU.
YOU ARE A TRAINED OFFICER, BUT I CAN SENSE YOUR FEAR.
I ASSUME THEY TAUGHT YOU: DO NOT DRAW YOUR WEAPON LESS YOU'RE PREPARED TO SHOOT.
I AM BEING COMPELLED TO SEE THAT NO HARM COMES TO YOU. STAND IN MY WAY AND I ASSURE YOU, THAT WILL CHANGE.
WHO ARE YOU AND WHAT HAVE YOU DONE WITH MY PARTNER?
DID YOU KNOW THAT YOU SNORE? QUITE LOUDLY, WHAT A NASTY HABIT, BEING WILLING TO ATTEMPT SLEEPING NEXT THAT KIND OF REST INTERRUPTION... ITS GOT TO BE LOVE.
JACK... IS THAT YOU?
VROOOM
LOOK OUT BEHIND YOU!

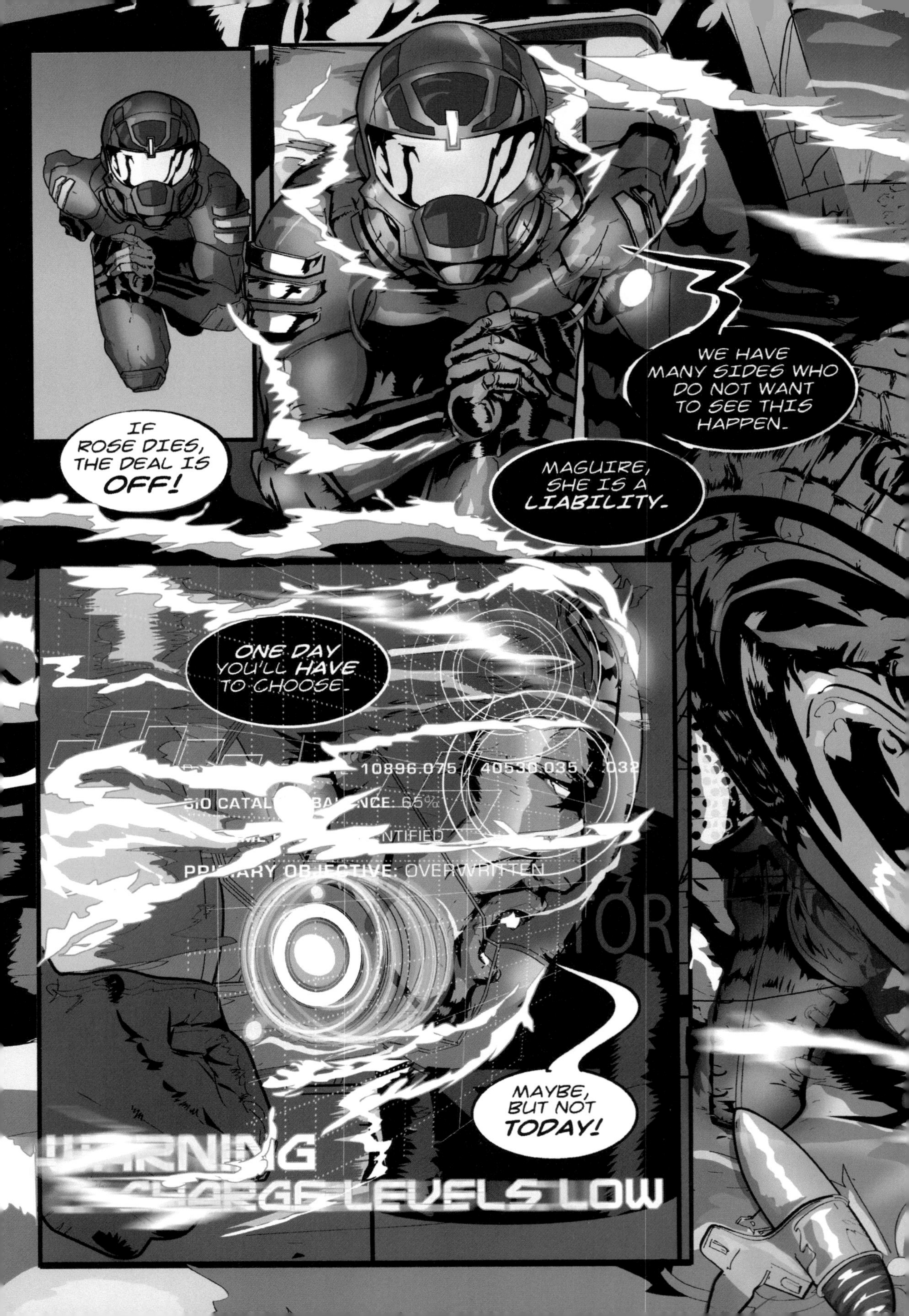
IF ROSE DIES, THE DEAL IS OFF!
WE HAVE MANY SIDES WHO DO NOT WANT TO SEE THIS HAPPEN.
MAGUIRE, SHE IS A LIABILITY.
ONE DAY YOU'LL HAVE TO CHOOSE.
10896.075 40530.035 .032
PRIMARY OBJECTIVE: OVERWRITTEN
MAYBE, BUT NOT TODAY!
LEVELS LOW

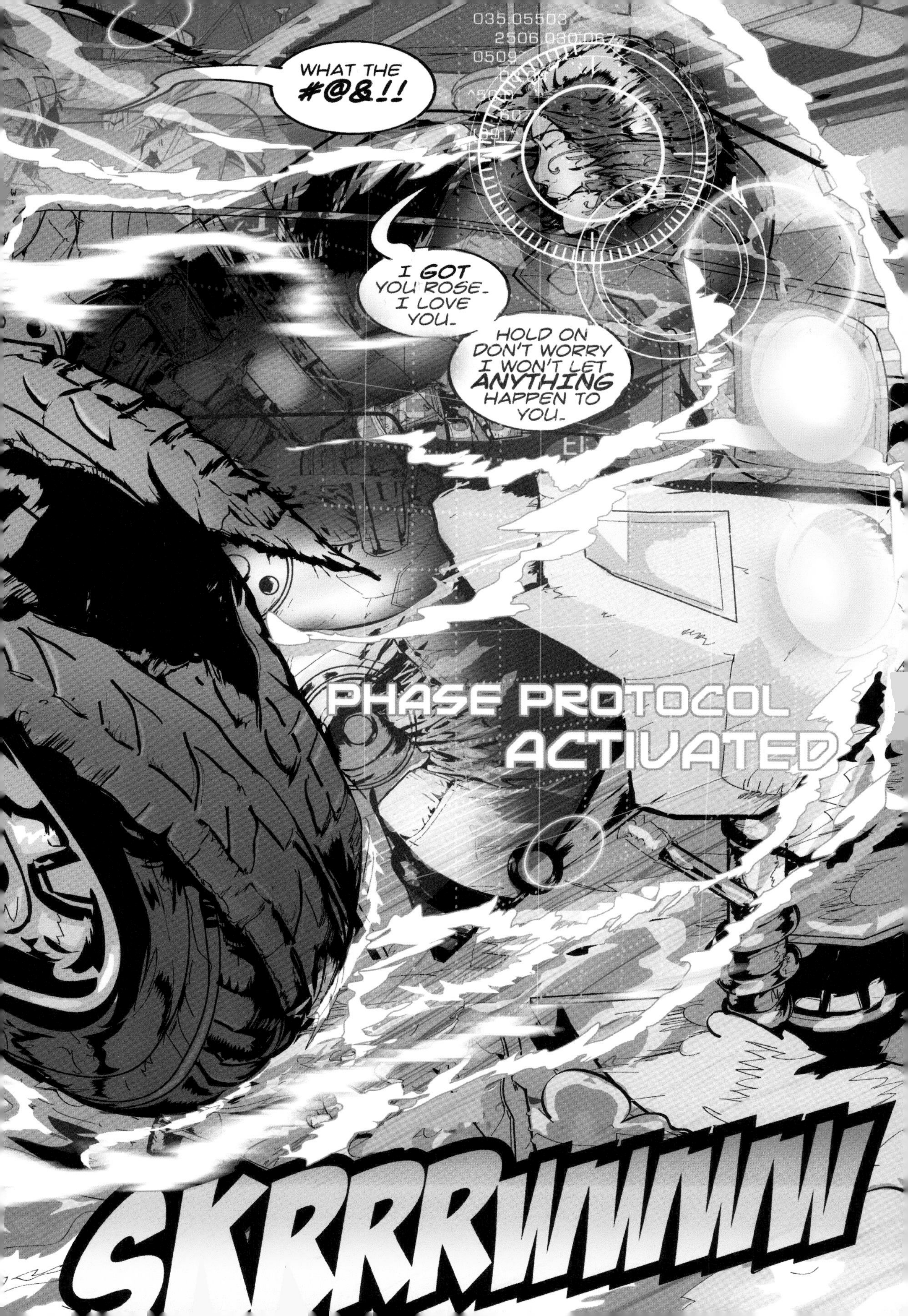
WHAT THE #@&!!
I GOT YOU ROSE. I LOVE YOU.
HOLD ON DON'T WORRY I WON'T LET ANYTHING HAPPEN TO YOU.
PHASE PROTOCOL ACTIVATED
SKRRRWWWWW

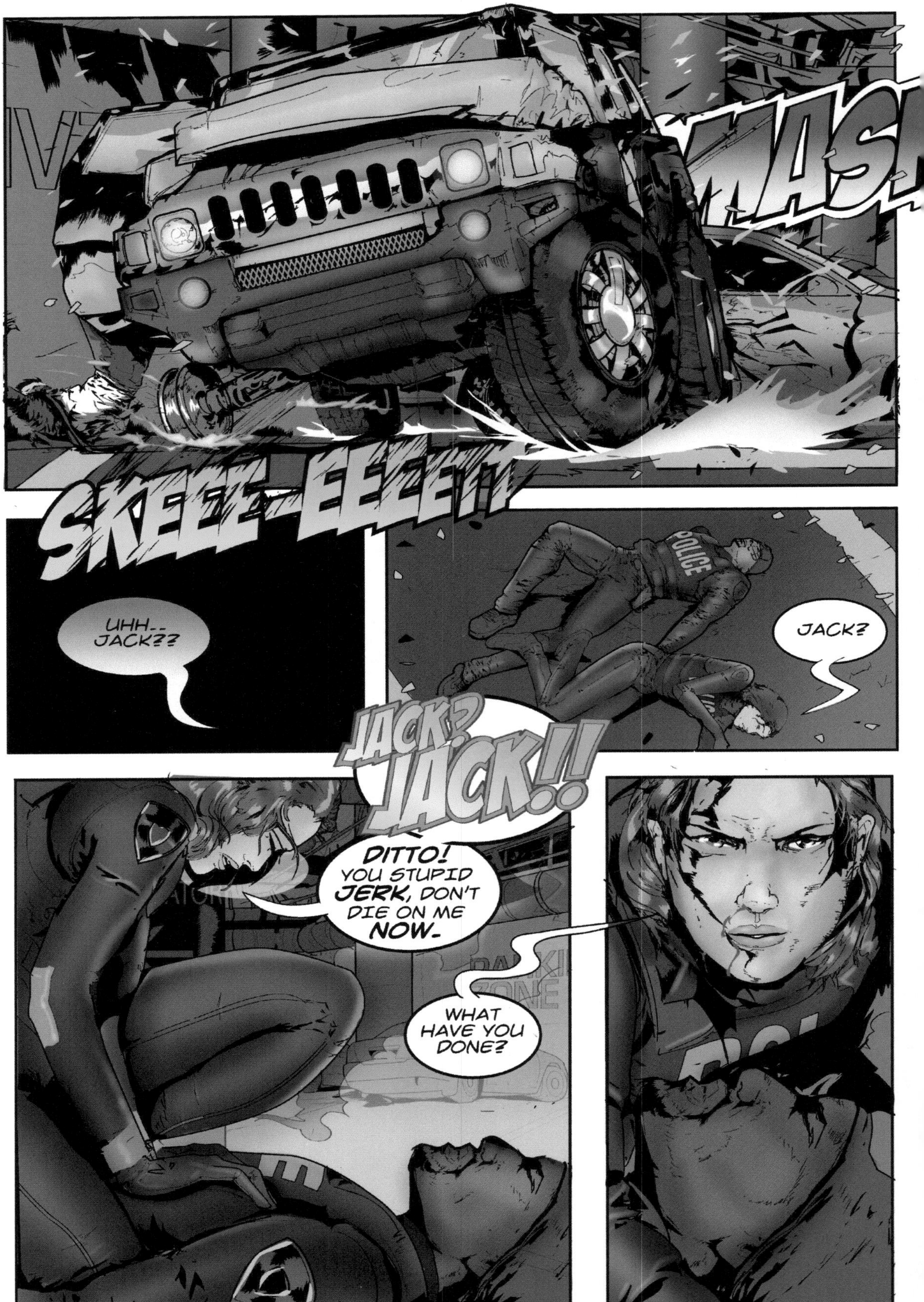

SKEEZ-EEEEE!!
UHH.. JACK??
JACK?
JACK? JACK!!
DITTO! YOU STUPID JERK, DON'T DIE ON ME NOW.
WHAT HAVE YOU DONE?

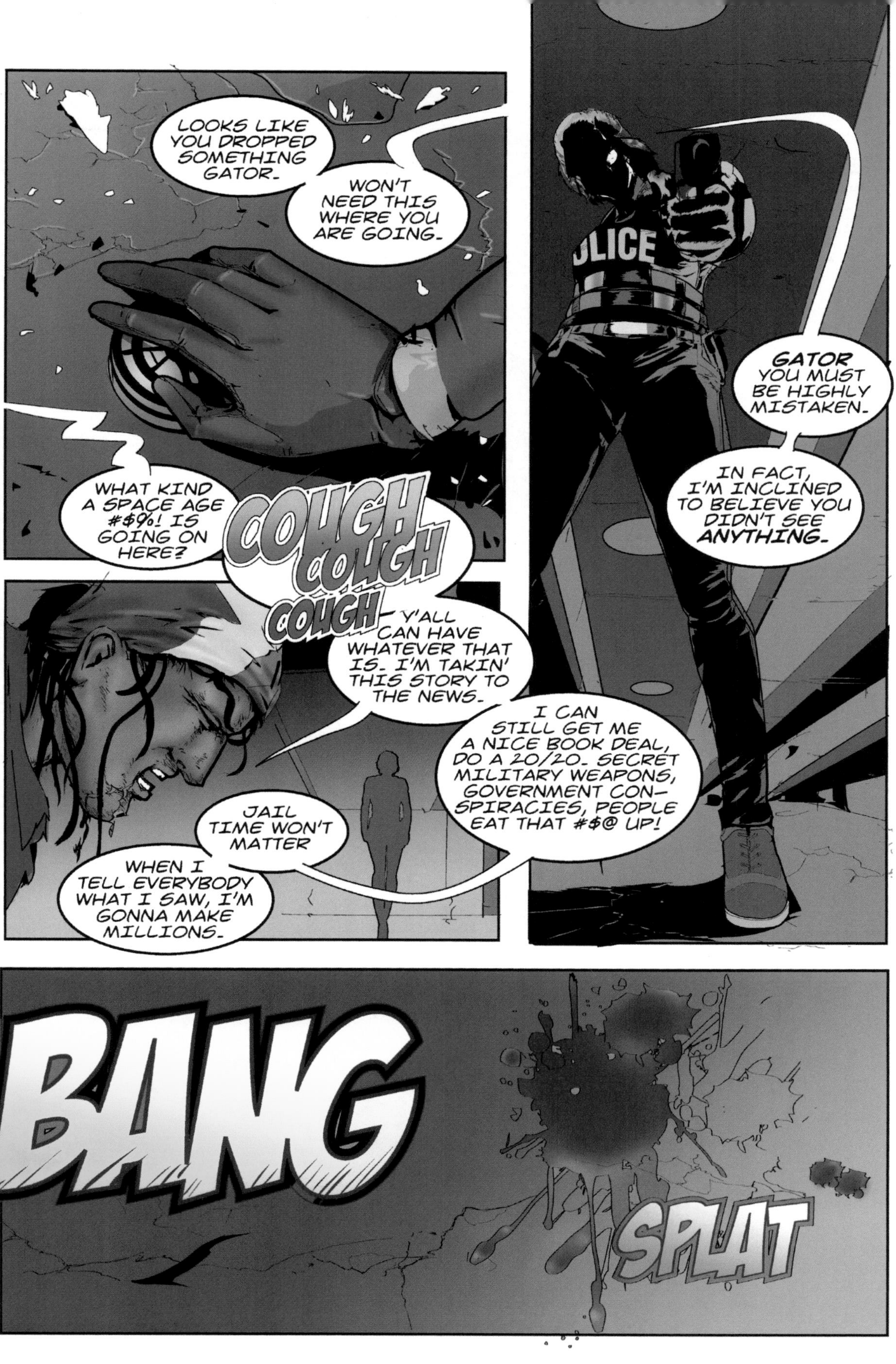

LOOKS LIKE YOU DROPPED SOMETHING GATOR.
WON'T NEED THIS WHERE YOU ARE GOING.
WHAT KIND A SPACE AGE #$%! IS GOING ON HERE?
COUGH COUGH COUGH
Y'ALL CAN HAVE WHATEVER THAT IS. I'M TAKIN' THIS STORY TO THE NEWS.
I CAN STILL GET ME A NICE BOOK DEAL, DO A 20/20. SECRET MILITARY WEAPONS, GOVERNMENT CONSPIRACIES, PEOPLE EAT THAT #$@ UP!
JAIL TIME WON'T MATTER
WHEN I TELL EVERYBODY WHAT I SAW, I'M GONNA MAKE MILLIONS.
LICE
GATOR YOU MUST BE HIGHLY MISTAKEN.
IN FACT, I'M INCLINED TO BELIEVE YOU DIDN'T SEE ANYTHING.
BANG
SPLAT

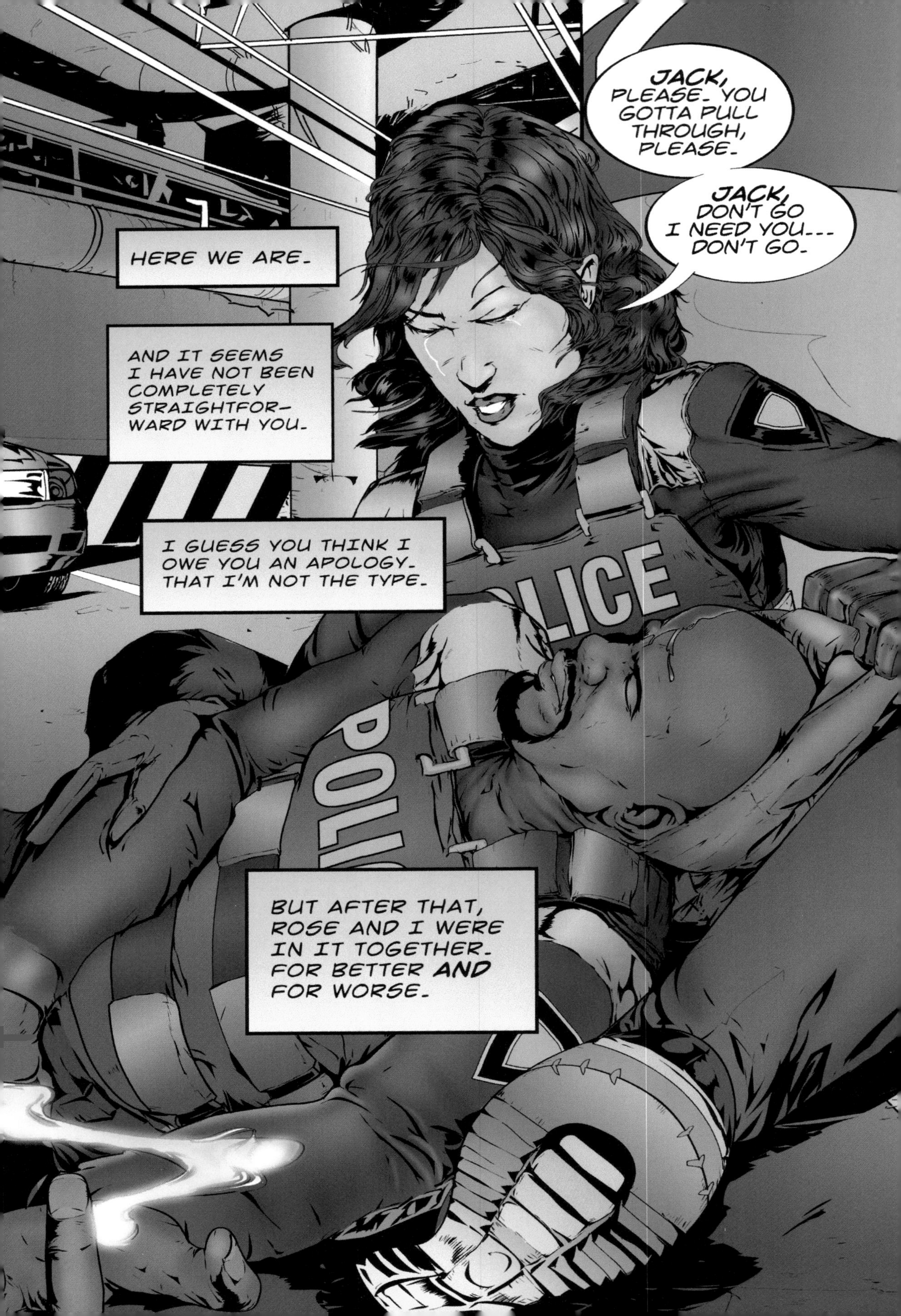
HERE WE ARE.
AND IT SEEMS I HAVE NOT BEEN COMPLETELY STRAIGHTFORWARD WITH YOU.
JACK, PLEASE. YOU GOTTA PULL THROUGH, PLEASE.
JACK, DON'T GO I NEED YOU... DON'T GO.
I GUESS YOU THINK I OWE YOU AN APOLOGY. THAT I'M NOT THE TYPE.
POLICE
POLICE
BUT AFTER THAT, ROSE AND I WERE IN IT TOGETHER. FOR BETTER AND FOR WORSE.

PRODUCER EXTRAORDINAIRE

Harrio

PRODUCERS

Sylvia	Hom
Belinda	Nieh
Michael	Ricart
Daniel	Eng
Mark	Lim
David	Wu
Liz	Reisch Picarazzi
R. S.	Randolph
Naomi	Dobrowolski

DEDICATED TO

My wonderful wife, Amy Tan Walford
and our three Rascals: Kayla, Charles & Colette
"Anything is possible."

IN LOVING MEMORY

Winston George Walford

THANK YOU

Anthony Greenwood	Jim Chonko	Jonathan Fung
Brad Dancer	Monty OoTG -	Gregory Kane
lostwhilecaching	Member of RS42	www.gnut.co.uk
Coniah Grimes	Peter Schnare	

GET THE DEBUT TITLE FROM FORWARD COMIX

NOWHERE MAN
YOU DON'T KNOW JACK
VOL. BOOK PROLOGUE + CHP
01.01:00-03
JEROME WALFORD

NOWHERE MAN
YOU DON'T KNOW JACK
VOL. BOOK CHAPTERS
01.02:04-07
JEROME WALFORD

NOWHERE MAN
YOU DON'T KNOW JACK
VOL. BOOK CHAPTERS
01.03:08-11
JEROME WALFORD

NOWHERE MAN VOLUME ONE: YOU DON'T KNOW JACK This series is a police drama and psychological thriller that will draw you in. Meet riveting characters on the verge of uncovering a web of secrets that will change their lives forever.

ALSO ARRIVING FROM FORWARD COMIX IN 2013

CURSE OF THE GRIFFIN
DANIEL'S PRIDE
A NOVEL BY JEROME WALFORD

CURSE OF THE GRIFFIN, DANIEL'S PRIDE.
Do you like vampires, gargoyles and other magical creatures? Here's your chance to see them all together in a compelling new novel.

comicart
artbook 2013

COMIC ART, 2013
If you enjoy collecting art books, be sure to add this little gem. "comic art" is a selected set of images from the best of Jerome Walford's work created from the summer of 2010 to the fall of 2012.

FORWARD COMIX

Great stories often crossover many genres, take us on wild adventures and various flights of fantasy. The best stories inspire us to move forward on the less frequented paths that lead to self discovery.

Forward Comix is an indie publisher based in Brooklyn New York. Our titles often mix various genres in the pursuit of something unique, our projects seek to capture the central timeless themes of the human spirit; hope, loss, struggle and redemption.

forwardcomix.com

/forwardcomix

@forwardcomix

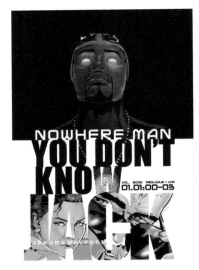

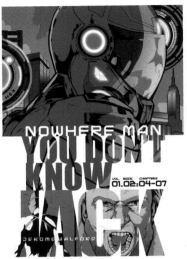

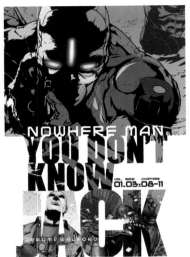

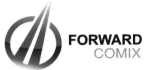

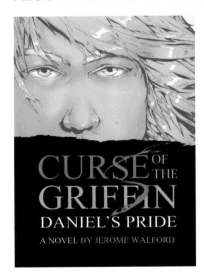

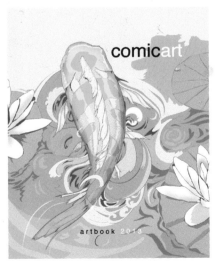

CPSIA information can be obtained
at www.ICGtesting.com
Printed in the USA
LVIW022307211212

312866LV00002B